Maren Muter

Soul Contract

MAREN MUTER

Soul CONTRACT

SIGN HERE_____

Soul Contract

Soul Contract

Author and Illustrator: Maren Muter

ISBN: 9798994089033

First Edition, 2026

Published independently by the author

Printed in the United States of America

Soul Contract

Soul Contract

Soul Contract

VIII

Note

I wrote this book eighteen weeks after being struck by lightning. The writing is basic and raw. Words following the lightning strike have been very hard to convey. I can hear them in my mind but speaking and writing them are another story entirely.

This is part of the challenge of recovery. And it brings me here to write and share along the way.

Thank you for reading,

Maren

Chapter One

The Paper Lantern Gospel

The first strike of the gong sent a tremor through the loft, rattling the dust on the skylight like a summons. The sound hovered for a moment before sinking into the heavy carpet and the silence of the yoga mats.

There were forty folding chairs arranged in a curve around a low table. On it, glass pitchers waited in a disciplined line, sweating clear droplets that crept toward the edge of the glass and released themselves, one by one, onto a woven runner. In the center, a Himalayan salt lamp sat like a piece of evidence, its orange glow deepening toward its core—the way moisture darkens a stone or ink settles into a page.

Molly took a seat near the center of the arc. She was close enough to observe the man at the front, but far enough back to avoid the front row, where she might be called upon without notice. She sat with the loose, hollow fatigue of a woman whose nights had been sheared into too many fractured segments.

Lena slid into the seat beside her. Her mason jar of green liquid knocked against her knee with a dull thud before she steadied it on the floor. The outside air had painted her nose and cheeks a rosey pink; she rubbed her palms together to warm up before resting them on her thighs.

"You made it," Lena whispered. "Your mom's going to light a candle about this."

Molly's mouth pulled into a thin line that passed for a smile. "She already did," she said, showing Lena the text. It was a string of praying hands and flowers, followed by: "Text me the play-by-play. I want to know what you think of Dr. Hart." Only, the "Hart" was represented by a pulsing red emoji.

In the corner, a fern performed a slow, rhythmic bow,

its longest frond grazing the floor in a passing draft.

Dr. Elian Hart stood at the front, his hands relaxed at his sides with the ease of a man who owned the room's jurisdiction. He wore a pale linen shirt and crisp trousers—the uniform of a high-end consultant for the spirit. The sunlight gathered along his shoulders and threaded through his light curls, resting there without hurry. A slim microphone curved along his jaw, though his voice possessed the natural resonance to reach the back of the room without any technical assistance.

"Welcome, soul family," he said.

The phrase moved through the room like a warm current. Shoulders unknotted; pens hovered over notebooks. A few people closed their eyes, drawing the words in as if they were a favorable verdict. His voice was a deep, safe baritone—the kind of voice that promised the fine print was in your favor.

Molly watched his mouth move. Each syllable arrived clean and deliberate. Her fingers traced the cool ridge of her water bottle out of habit. Her body ached for a reason, for a frame that would put the chaos of her life into an orderly ledger.

"We're here to remember why we came," Hart continued. "Not to this workshop, but to this lifetime. We are here to review the contracts we made. The people we chose. The challenges we volunteered for."

On an easel beside him, a poster displayed pastel silhouettes perched on clouds, looking down at a cartoon Earth with pens poised above scrolls.

REMEMBER YOUR SACRED CONTRACTS

Molly's mother had sent the flyer three times, a persistent subpoena of hope. "Molly, you must meet Dr. Hart. He can put things into context for you. It is better than hope, darling."

The word hope hummed behind every chair in the room. It was the currency of the loft.

"Before birth," Hart said, "we meet with our guides. We lay out a game plan. Families, partners, even the pain-points. Nothing is random. Nothing is wasted."

Molly's throat tightened. The idea brushed against a raw place inside her—a place that had spent too many nights asking "why" into the dark until the question itself began to fray.

Lena leaned close. "Watch his hands," she whispered. "He's dreamy."

Hart's hands moved like a conductor's, tracing arcs in the air that seemed to connect the two sides of the horseshoe. The gestures calmed more than dazzled, the way a doctor's precise movements steady a patient before a procedure.

"Imagine a conversation before you arrive into this life," he said. "'Next time, let's meet as siblings. Or as that stranger who changes everything.' You and your companions mapping intersections, coordinating growth for mutual benefit."

Soft laughter rippled through the chairs. It was the

sound of a room finally feeling the weight of the world lift.

A woman in the front row raised her hand, her hair streaked with lavender. "Do nightmare exes count? Because if I signed up for that one, I want to know what I was drinking on that cloud."

The laughter opened up then, genuine and collective. It gave everyone permission to breathe.

"Absolutely," Hart said with a warm smile. "Our most triggering relationships are often tied to the most important agreements. On a soul level, those exes love you enough to press your buttons. They volunteer to mirror your patterns so you can see them."

The word love, framed like that, felt like a physical warmth trying to share Molly's chair. Her fingers slipped from her water bottle; it hit the floor with a sharp, metallic clang.

"Sorry," she whispered, scrambling to set it upright.

On the table, the condensation from the nearest

pitcher finally reached the edge and dropped, darkening the fibers of the runner. The woven pattern swallowed the mark instantly.

"Many of you already sense this," Hart said, moving past the interruption with practiced ease. "Those relationships that felt destined—the child you waited for, the friend who appeared in your darkest hour. Those are all agreements in action."

Lena's pen moved fast across her notebook, drawing a small heart in the margin.

"We'll share some of those stories in a few minutes," he added. "The joyful ones. The miracles. Then we'll turn toward the harder agreements. The ones that challenge us to our core."

Imperceptibly, the air shifted. A faint resinous scent seeped from the diffuser in the corner; frankincense wound itself through recycled heating, through breath, through cloth.

Challenging agreements. The Olympic Rings formed in Molly's imagination, people on the awards stand getting metals for bravery.

Hart stepped closer to the salt lamp and rested his palm on it. Light pooled under his hand, deepening the orange where skin met stone.

"Sometimes," he said, "a soul chooses to experience rejection, illness, betrayal, even abuse, in order to grow compassion and self-worth. Another soul agrees—out of love—to play the difficult role. Onstage, pain. Off-stage, devotion."

The word abuse entered the room and stayed near the ceiling, unwilling to sit. It walked up to the Olympians on the podium, shoved its way past third, second, and pushed first off.

A car horn wailed out on the street, then cut off. Molly's mind went back to her mother's voice: "We're brave souls, you and I. We signed up to heal this together."

Hart continued. "On the human level, harm remains unacceptable. On the soul level, we explore the possibility that even the darkest moments contain threads of agreement and growth."

She watched his face, searching for any flinch, any crack. But, none surfaced. His eyes remained clear, intent on his message.

"Take a breath," he instructed. "Notice what moves inside you as you, the expansion of your rib cage, and your belly. Let your breath out, how does it feel? Consider this frame of breath."

Chairs creaked as people shifted. Some inhaled on cue. Bracelets chimed in tiny notes along the semicircle.

Molly drew air in through her nose. Lavender, salt, the soaps and perfumes of those around her. The breath met a hard knot under her sternum and pressed against it.

Her mother had framed abandonment as curriculum. Electricity shutoffs, empty fridges, men who arrived and evaporated—everything tucked into the same sentence: We signed up to heal this, you and I.

Molly had wanted to believe it. Wanted the universe to be that orderly. Wanted pain to attach to purpose instead of accident.

Hart clapped once, quietly.

"Let's meet each other," he said. "We'll form small circles, share our names, and name one relationship that feels destined in a nourishing way. A child, an animal, a friend, a love. No pressure for depth yet. What soulmates have you met?"

Chairs scraped softly across the floor. The horseshoe reshaped into eight bubbles of five. Lena pivoted toward Molly, knees angled in, making room for the others who joined them.

A woman in a floral dress spoke first. "I'm Carrie," she said. "My daughter's my soul contract. I had three miscarriages before her and the doctors gave up. Then she arrived. No explanation. I know we promised each other."

Heads nodded in appreciation. The man beside her—tattoos across his knuckles, denim jacket worn at the elbows—cleared his throat.

"I'm DeShawn," he said. "My grandma, definitely. I tried hard to wreck myself in my twenties. Every time, she pulled me back with one sentence from a song, of all things. I still hear her. After she died, strangers started singing her hymn around me. Random places. Grocery store, on the bus, once at the dentist's office."

The hairs along Molly's arms lifted. A hum threaded through the group, shared recognition of pattern.

"What a beautiful guardian contract," Hart said, coming up to their group. "Soul anchors."

Lena's turn came. She tucked hair behind one ear, fingers trembling for half a second and looked at her notebook.

"I'm Lena," she said. "My sister and I...we clash. All the time. But every breakthrough in my life lines up with some crisis of hers and visa versa. It's like we take turns falling apart and dragging each other up, out of the muck. I don't know what we signed, but I am glad we did."

When Lena was done, the eyes shifted toward Molly.

She wet her lips. "Molly," she said. Her own name sounded foreign in her mouth. "My mother, I think?"

The group waited.

"She believes in soul contracts more than anyone I know. She says I chose her before I had a body. That we agreed to burn through old karma together this round." Her stomach filled with champaign bubbles as she spoke. "We've been through a lot together, but also not much. Just life, I suppose."

"Do you believe her?" Hart asked.

Heat crept along the back of her neck. The ceiling fan blades spun above, insistently asking with each rotation, do you? Do you? Do you?

"On good days," Molly said, "it comforts me. On bad days, it feels like a spiritual version of, 'you made your bed, now lie in it.'"

"Both reactions make sense," Hart said. "Part of you hears the promise of meaning. Another part protests being blamed for what hurt you. That tension deserves respect. And once you realize you agreed to the hurt, it takes the pressure off as you take responsibility for your part."

His eyes locked into hers like a soft palm on her shoulder.

The circle moved on: a dog who slept only on the side of the bed a departed partner once occupied; a neighbor who arrived with food on the exact day a woman lost her job. Each story clicked into the framework Hart offered. Each coincidence folded into design.

Across the room, a row of candles burned on a narrow shelf under the window. Their flames rose straight and calm—except one. That wick guttered and flared in short, frantic bursts. Wax pooled thick around its base, swallowing the stem. The flame fought for air while its neighbors burned without struggle.

When the sharing wound down, and the chairs

returned to the lucky horseshoe, Hart stood again at the front.

"You can feel the pattern," he said. "Threads crossing at precise moments. Support arriving when old agreements ripen. Your lives contain more orchestration than your rational minds admit."

Acknowledgment moved through the room in small gestures: a hand against a heart, a slow exhale, a whisper to a friend.

"But," he continued, "as some of you already sensed, not all agreements feel kind. Some souls take on harder roles, deeper shadows. We'll explore those with great care as we go. Especially in our private sessions."

His gaze flicked briefly toward the side table near the door, where clipboards waited. Lists for FOLLOW-UP COURSE, ONE-ON-ONE REGRESSION, VOLUNTEER SUPPORT TEAM. A small bowl of polished mantra stones sat beside them. TRUST. SURRENDER. COURAGE. CLARITY.

"For now," Hart said, "we keep our focus on support. On the ways your agreements have already held you. Let that awareness strengthen your nervous system before we step into tougher terrain."

He led them through a short closing. Palm to touch and follow each chakra. The gong sounded in closing a tone that rolled through the room and settled beneath their feet.

Chairs scraped as people rose. Lena caught Molly's wrist.

"Come sign up," she said, already moving toward the table. "He opened a few regression slots this week, then he's booked out for months. You have to grab one."

The thought of lying down in an office with his voice guiding her into old scenes sparked both longing and unease. Her nights had turned into a revolving door of restless images anyway. At least a guided descent promised structure. A witness. A hand on the railing, sort of speak.

"Lena…" Molly began. "I don't know."

"You told me you wanted this," Lena said quietly. "Not him, necessarily. The answers. A frame that makes sense of what you went through. You don't have to love the language. You can translate later. But you can't keep doing the insomnia thing forever."

The words landed without accusation. A simple observation.

Hart stood a few feet away, speaking with a couple about dreams that warned them before accidents. Up close, the faint lines around his eyes deepened when he smiled. No gleam of triumph, no sharp edge. Only attentiveness that read as genuine.

Molly's pulse thudded at the base of her throat. Her mind replayed the image he'd offered: souls around a table made of dark, deciding roles before birth. Her mother reaching across that table with a hand that shook and still reached anyway. Hers meeting it.

"If this is real," she said under her breath, "I should know."

Lena pressed a pen into her hand. "Then ask," she said. "You don't have to keep guessing in the dark."

The paper waited. Lines for names. Columns for email, phone, preferred days. The black tip of the pen hovered above the first blank space.

A part of her wanted to step back, guard the last territory of not knowing. Another part leaned forward, hungry for any map, even one drawn in symbols she might contest later.

Ink met paper. Her name took shape in her handwriting—Molly Ellison—letters steady despite the thrum in her veins.

The snake plant's tallest leaf trembled, a barely visible shiver as someone opened the door to leave.

When she returned the clipboard to the stack, the word on the stone nearest her elbow caught her eye. CLARITY, etched into rose quartz. Her fingers closed around it before she could argue with herself and placed it in her pocket.

Hart's conversation ended. He moved toward the table and paused before her.

"I'm glad you're joining us for regression work," he said. "You carry depth. The agreements around that are often intricate. We'll explore with those with care."

Warmth entered his voice on the word care in a way that brushed against the sore edges inside her.

Behind him, the salt lamp deepened in color.

In her pocket, the quartz cooled her palm, then warmed against her skin.

"See you Tuesday," Hart said.

Chapter Two

The Lake of Doors

Molly arrived early for the regression.

The hallway outside Hart's office gathered the morning in a muted hush, a soft winter light drifting through frosted glass, eucalyptus from the diffuser mingling with the faint trace of someone's citrus lotion. A small water feature in the corner released its rhythm, one ripple at a time. The sound steadied her nervous energy.

Her sleep had fractured again. Images surfaced through the night like debris rising from a dark lake—shapes without name, thresholds without hinges. She woke with the ache of a question, sharp and insistent. Answers felt close, just beneath reach, as if the world pressed a message against her skin and waited for her to open.

The office door opened with a dry click. "Come in," Hart said.

He stood aside while she crossed the threshold. Light from the tall window settled around him, softening the edges of his frame. The room breathed with plants—broad leaves in clay pots, tendrils trailing down shelves, a few stems angled toward her as she entered, as though scenting her arrival.

"You're early," he greeted her.

"I didn't want to rush," Molly said.

"Please, have a seat." His hand brushed the back of the armchair in invitation. "Regression asks the body for trust. So, we will begin slowly. Kind of like a first kiss."

She lowered herself into the chair. The cushion welcomed her weight with a quiet sigh. On the table beside her, the bowl of stones from the sign-up table glimmered—amethyst, rose quartz, black tourmaline, engravements introducing themselves again. Her fingers drifted across the rim, hesitating over another stone that said CLARITY before moving on.

Hart settled across from her, notebook closed, pen untouched. "Before we begin," he said, "tell me what brought you here beyond your mother's enthusiasm, and Lena's encouragement."

Heat crept up Molly's throat. She inhaled the room—earth from the soil, the cool tang of eucalyptus, fabric warmed by sunlight.

"I haven't been sleeping," she said. "Most nights I wake-up every hour. I wake with this…pressure. Anxiety, maybe. But, maybe, more like a door opening somewhere behind my eyes."

Hart's gaze held steady. "Does the door lead anywhere?"

Her fingers tightened around the arm of the chair. "Not yet. But something's there. Something is behind it, I just know it."

He nodded once, slow. "That's often how agreements surface. Not as memories. As invitations."

She reached for the water cup on the table. The glass cooled her palm. She didn't take a drink.

"I want to understand what's happening," Molly said. "If there's a pattern. If there's meaning to the timing. I don't want to keep circling the same things over and over again."

"You don't strike me as someone who circles," Hart said. "You strike me as someone who advances when she senses a path."

"Well, it doesn't seem like advancing, Dr. Hart." She swallowed once, throat tight. "It is stagnant. Dead. Water. A repeat."

He leaned forward slightly. "Regression is about giving you access to material your conscious mind protects. You'll remain aware, able to speak, able to stop if anything overwhelms you. But you may encounter images or sensations from deeper layers of memory or agreement. Not all are literal. Some are symbolic. But all useful. Do you understand that?"

Molly nodded.

"Good," he said. "Before we begin, I want to ask something delicate. Have you ever questioned your mother's interpretation of your connection?"

Molly's breath drew shallow. "Yes," she said. "But not because I don't believe we're connected. I mean, because, obviously we are. She gave birth to me. But I just have a hard time understanding why, why are these agreements made? Why must I do them? Can I change them? But how can I change them if I don't know what they are?"

Hart's hands rested on his knees, open. "Well, it is easier than you think to find what your agreements are. Every moment of your life is the agreement. So, today we explore what belongs to you. And only you."

Why that made her uneasy, she didn't know. But, what she did know was she was tired of feeling rubbish.

"Let's begin with grounding," he said. "Then we'll explore the door you mentioned."

He guided her through breath—slow inhale, slower re-lease. The world narrowed to sensation: the weight of her body, the grain of fabric beneath her fingers, the light pressing through her closed lids. Her heart-beat softened under the rhythm.

"Good," Hart murmured. "Now let your attention drift toward that door."

The image surfaced immediately—a dark outline against deeper dark, a frame without hinges or han-dle. The same shape that haunted her nights. Pres-sure pulsed behind her sternum as though her ribs had thinned around it.

"Stay with it," he said. "You're doing well."

The room dimmed behind her closed eyes. The door brightened in contrast, its edges gaining texture—rough, uneven, wood swollen by time or water.

24

Her breath skipped.

"What do you notice?" His voice stayed low, a steady tether.

"The wood," she whispered. "It…holds moisture. Like it's been underwater."

"Is it open?"

"No."

"Do you want it open?"

A tremor moved through her wrist, sharp as cold.

"Umm. Yes. I think."

"Tell it."

The air around her ribs tightened. Phosphorescent particles gathered along the door's seams, faint as breath against glass. She sensed something behind it—not hostile, not benevolent. Waiting. Patient.

The image flickered. Her pulse knocked at her throat.

She gripped the armrest. The cushion dented under her fingers.

"Molly," Hart said, voice closer now. "Stay with your breath. In… out. Good. What's happening?"

"It's too bright behind the door," she whispered.

"Brightness can be intensity, not danger. If it moves toward you, let it. You're not alone here."

Heat pooled at the base of her spine. Her shoulders curled forward.

Then—

An image broke through: her childhood hallway, shadowed, walls the color of wet stone. A single bulb burned at the far end, swaying without wind. A metallic tang, sharp on her tongue bit into her.

Her eyelids stung.

"Molly?" Hart's voice steadied her. "Where are you now?"

"A hallway," she breathed. "Mine. From childhood."

"Is the door there too?"

"Yes."

"Good. You can choose how close to get to it."

She took one slow step inside the memory. The floor-boards beneath her mental feet groaned—a sound too precise to dismiss as invention. Something in the house watched through the grain of the wood, attentive, patient as building hunger.

Her breath fractured.

"Molly," Hart said. "Come back to the chair for a moment."

She obeyed the sound of his voice like a rope thrown through darkness. Her attention snapped back to her body—the warmth under her thighs, the cool air brushing her collarbone.

Her eyes opened. The room steadied around her.

Plants angled toward her again, as though tracking her return. The salt lamp glowed deeper now, almost amber.

Hart studied her with a quiet focus. "You touched something important."

She nodded, throat dry. She placed her hand into her pocket, to the stone in her pocket—the rose quartz she'd taken from the table.

CLARITY.

Her finger traced the engraving.

He reached for a folder near his chair, sliding out a sheet on a clipboard. "Before you go, I'll need you to look over the consent form. Regression can stir dormant material. Temporary emotional distress, vivid dreams, spontaneous recall. None of this means harm. It means access."

Molly accepted the clipboard.

The paper crackled under her hands. Words rose from the page, temporary dissociation, resurfacing

28

imagery, somatic memory activation. The language should have frightened her. Instead it steadied in her.

"Read carefully," Hart said. "This work opens long agreements. Your system needs to know you're choosing this."

She read every line. And Signed.

When she returned the clipboard, his fingers brushed hers. She pulled away bumping into the bowl of stones. One stone struck the rim, and settled with a soft collision against a black tourmaline engraved with BOUNDARIES.

Goosebumps clamored her arms.

Hart's gaze caught the movement. A small nod followed, approving. "Boundaries are not walls," he said. "They're doorframes. They define where passage occurs. We'll continue in our next session," Hart said. "Your agreements are waking. Write everything down, even fragments of memory that comes to you."

Molly held the quartz like a security blanket.

"Thank you," she said.

"Tuesday," Hart answered. "Be ready, we'll go deeper."

She stepped into the hallway. The diffuser released another ribbon of eucalyptus, cool and clean. The water feature whispered at her ankles.

Behind the closed door, the "something" shifted—like wood settling, or a hinge adjusting itself in anticipation.

Chapter Three

The Descent Room

The building stood as a sentry.

Molly paused at the top of the stairwell leading to the lower floor, fingertips grazing the cool metal rail. She looked at the stairs, and tried to encourage her feet to move. "I don't know if I want to do this." She whispered to the little houseplant by the exterior door. Light from above faltered through the dust specks.

She looked again at Lena's had text from earlier: You'll be fine. Trust the process.

Fine, she thought and went down the stairs. Following the corridor, the carpet softened her steps. Hart's office waited at the end, a single line of amber light spilling across the hallway like a path pulled tight through the open door.

Inside, the room had changed.

The reclining chair sat in the center, angled toward the window, and a low bench beside it. The curtains draped heavy framing the window.

"Welcome," Hart said, striding towards her, giving her a casual hug. And, with a slight push from his foot, he closed the door. The latch settled into place with a soft, click.

"You rearranged the room," Molly said, voice quieter than she intended.

"For this regression, I thought we would create a vessel," he said. "Fewer objects. Fewer distractions. More room for the unseen."

Her pulse edged upward. She stepped toward the recliner. The plants on the shelves tracked her again—leaves turning, subtle but certain, responding to her movement.

"Have you been sleeping since our last session?" Hart asked.

"Not really, but when I do I have more dreams," she answered. "Not restful ones by any means."

He nodded. "That's common when agreements stir. Your dreams become thresholds, not noise, you'll see."

Molly approached the reclining chair.

"What surfaced in the dreams?" Hart asked.

She searched for a shape, a color, a single clean image to anchor the answer, but memory swam in fragments—the hallway from her childhood, the door swelling with brightness, the sensation of standing ankle-deep in cold water though no water showed.

"A presence," she said. "Behind the door."

Hart's gaze deepened, attentive. "Then we go to it. We make contact with the frame."

He gestured toward the chair.

Molly lowered herself into it. The fabric enveloped her shoulders. Her spine eased into the curve. Breath rose and fell in the tight cadence of anticipation.

Hart pulled a woven blanket across her ankles, grounding the weight. "Tell me if this feels too warm," he murmured.

"It's good."

He dimmed the lights, leaving only a thin seam of daylight that slipped under the curtain. The room settled into an amber half-dark, shadow pooling in corners like ink gathering before a stroke.

"Close your eyes," he said. She obeyed.

His voice shifted into the cadence from their first session, low and rhythmic. "Inhale through the belly. Exhale through the ribs. Good. Let your breath rise through your throat, then soften. Let your body sink."

Her limbs loosened. Light behind her eyelids reddened and darkened. The air warmed against her skin

34

as if the room itself leaned closer.

"Go to the door," Hart said, "but stay on your side of it. Nothing opens without your consent."

Darkness stirred in front of her. The door materialized—grain swelling, wood bruised with age, edges blurred by humidity. A faint shimmer traced its outline.

Her breath froze.

"What do you see?" Hart murmured.

"The door," she whispered. "Same wood. There's water inside it."

"Step toward it."

She did. The boards beneath her feet creaked—the exact pitch of the hallway from childhood. The sound scraped along a buried place in her memory, unsettling the air in her lungs.

Behind the door, something shifted, not water now.

A pressure pulsed outward.

Molly's pulse tightened. "It's aware of me," she said.

"Awareness is not harm," Hart answered. "Stay with it."

A white glow seeped through the cracks, then it became tinged with gold her body recognized before her mind caught up. Her chest warmed as though a hand pressed there from inside.

The brightness bulged. The door trembled.

Her knees weakened inside the memory. "It wants me to open it."

Hart's voice stayed steady, quiet. "You don't open anything today. You only listen. Agreements speak before they are revealed."

The brightness surged again, brighter this time—too bright, almost metallic. The air in front of her thickened. Her throat closed halfway.

"Molly?" Hart's voice reached through. "Where is

your breath?"

She dragged air in. Her chest constricted, ribs trembling around the inhale.

"Good. Anchor in the chair."

The scent of the room pressed back against the memory.

"Describe what the door holds," Hart said.

"It's a memory." Her voice thinned. "Something from childhood."

"Is it yours?"

"Yes."

"Does it pull you toward pain or recognition?"

Her jaw clenched. Fingertips curled against the blanket. The brightness behind the door shook its head reminding her not to tell their secret, "this is ours." The light began to flicker like a candle struggling to survive its own heat.

"Recognition," she whispered. "But I don't know what it recognizes."

Hart touched her silently. She did not open her eyes—the displacement of air, the shift of warmth, the soft creak of floorboards beneath his weight.

"When you're ready," he said, "touch the door. Only with your mind. A graze, nothing more."

Her hand in the memory lifted. The wood waited, swollen with desire now, glistening with moisture. A faint vibration passed through its surface, like breath behind it.

Her fingertips brushed the grain.

A sound cracked through the darkness—a single, sharp knock. The room jerked around her. Her eyes flew open.

The sound had not come from the memory.

It had come from the physical door of Hart's office.

Hart straightened, expression unreadable. He turned

toward the doorway. Shadows shifted in the corridor beyond the frosted glass—an indistinct shape, then nothing.

"Stay here," he said softly.

He crossed the room, opened the door a few inches, and looked into the hallway. Silence pooled behind the threshold. No footsteps. No voices.

He closed the door again, slower this time, as though the wood needed reassurance.

"False alarm," he said. "Go back to breath."

But the knock lingered in Molly's bones, scratching at her ribs. The presence behind her internal door responded with a faint surge, as though it had heard the interruption and was almost caught.

"You're safe," Hart said.

She tried to settle. The blanket warmed her shins. The air thickened with eucalyptus again.

Her eyes closed.

The door in the memory stood closer now, uncomfortably near—as if she had lost distance without taking a step. The shimmer along its edges intensified.

"What changed?" Hart asked, voice low.

"It moved," she whispered.

"Doors don't move on their own. Something behind it may be reaching. That doesn't mean danger. It may be eager. You decide whether to step back."

Molly stepped backward in the memory. The door followed.

Her breath halted. A cold ribbon slid down her spine. "I want to stop," she said.

"Then stop," Hart answered immediately. His voice tightened with new gravity. "Open your eyes."

She opened them. The world reassembled in segments: plant leaves angled toward her, curtain rip-pling once without breeze, Hart kneeling beside her chair, his hand on her forearm.

"You did well," he said, patting her. "You made contact with an early layer. Whatever moved behind the door knew you were there."

A tremor passed through the chair as her body released tension. Her palms dampened the fabric.

"Why did it move like that?" she asked.

"Some agreements hold urgency," he said. "Not danger—urgency. They wake when you approach the truth too slowly for their design."

Her pulse stuttered.

"Drink," he said, offering the glass.

She lifted it. Water kissed her lips, cool at first, then warmer as it slid down her throat. Her chest steadied.

"We'll stop here for today," Hart said. "Your system signaled it has had enough. Your dreams tonight may sharpen. Don't ignore any detail."

She nodded.

He helped her sit fully upright.

Molly steadied her breath. The knock still pulsed faintly inside her sternum.

"Next session," Hart said, "we go deeper—but only with your full permission. A door like that rarely belongs to surface memory. It leads to a core agreement."

She rose on unsteady legs.

As she crossed the room, the salt lamp brightened again. The amber core ignited for a moment, color deepened to a shade close to bloodstone.

Hart opened the door for her. The hallway looked normal—fluorescent light steady, carpet undisturbed. No sign of the intrusion.

Yet the air in the corridor pressed against her, cooler, aware. "Tuesday," Hart said behind her. "We'll continue."

The door closed behind her. The wood settled.

Chapter Four

Sacred Villains

Rain started before dawn. By noon, gutters pulled a gray slurry of water and leaf pulp toward the drains. Traffic lights smeared red and green across the slick asphalt. Tires dragged a low, constant growl along the street that pressed against office windows.

Molly sat in front of her dual monitors, cursor blinking in a field of unfinished code. Lines of characters blurred into each other. In the gaps between keystrokes, other images surfaced: the river that moved without banks, the invisible shiver of energy, Ren, placed its hand over hers on the stone - a presence from the valley that felt more like her than anyone else, the contract hall carved from light, that pause at twelve where time waited for a choice.

At three, a new email slid into her inbox.

Subject: Integration Circle – Tough Love Agreements

From: info@hartintegrative.com

She opened it.

Dear Molly,

For clients currently in regression work, I host a small integration group on Wednesdays at seven.

Tonight's focus: Tough Love Soul Agreements – Case Studies in Sacred Villain Roles.

We discuss how souls collaborate through challenging contracts, including abuse, illness, and loss. Hearing others' journeys often supports understanding of one's own.

RSVP not required. Attend as you feel called. With care,

Elian

Sacred villains. The phrase moved along her tongue with a metallic edge.

Outside, rain tapped the glass harder, a tempo shift that carried impatience.

Molly closed her laptop at six-thirty. The office lights washed the cubicles in flat white; everyone else had already drifted home or into other routines. She slipped on her coat. The stone in her pocket brushed her hip—CLARITY—its familiar weight tracking each step she took toward the elevator.

The integration circle met in a smaller room than the original workshop. Carpet hushed sound underfoot. Two lamps in the corners wore mandala-print shades, casting patterned shadows across the ceiling.

Chairs formed a tight ring. Seven bodies already occupied some of them: a man in a worn sports hoodie, curls silvering at the edges; the woman whose mascara had run at the previous group; a young woman with a buzz cut and a spider lily tattoo blooming across her throat; a tall person in an oversized black sweater; two older women pressed hip-to-hip; a slender man with headphones resting around his neck, fingers working a beaded bracelet without pause.

Hart stood near a portable whiteboard. Across the top he had written, in the same measured handwriting as the workshop:

TOUGH LOVE & SACRED VILLAINS

A spider plant perched on a filing cabinet beside him. Long striped leaves spilled over the edge.

"Welcome," he said. "Glad you made it through the weather." Water clung to coats, hair, lashes. Droplets slid down cheeks and jawlines, not emotion yet, only climate.

He inclined his head when Molly chose an empty chair. A greeting in his gaze, steady and warm.

"This circle holds clients in active regression work," he said. "We share experiences, questions, integration. Everything spoken here stays here."

A soft murmur traveled the ring.

"Tonight," he continued, tapping the board, "we explore contracts that involve darker roles. People who act as 'villains' in our lives—abusers, betrayers, abandoners. From the soul vantage, many volunteered for those parts before incarnation. The intention: accelerated growth, balancing of karmic currents, service to the whole."

The word abusers dropped into the room with dense weight. The spider plant sank one leaf a fraction lower, its tip dragging along the cabinet's icy surface.

Hart picked up a small black flashlight from the table beside him. He switched it on; the beam angled against his open palm.

"Imagine a theater," he said. "House lights dim. A villain strides onstage and commits terrible acts. The audience reacts. After the show, backstage, the actor and cast embrace, laugh, praise each other's dedication. No real harm transfers between the souls behind the masks."

Light slid along his fingers. Shadows lengthened on the wall.

"On Earth," he said, "we forget the backstage. We only experience the role. That forgetting intensifies the lesson. Souls draft these roles together in pre-birth councils—'This time, I push you hard. I step into shadow so you can meet your power.' Those choices arise from profound love."

Mascara Woman hugged her canvas bag against her chest. "My ex," she said, voice raw around the edges. "Elian helped me see our contract. I carried so much rage. Through the sessions, I saw how his addiction and cruelty aligned with my soul's request to break patterns. On the highest level, he loved me more than anyone else ever did."

More than anyone else. Heat crept along Molly's spine at the phrase.

"Thank you, Brie," Hart said. "Your willingness to re-frame such tenderness and hurt offers strong medicine."

He looked around the circle. "Who else has an example of a sacred villain, and how viewing the relationship that way shifted your inner landscape?"

Buzz Cut hesitated, then lifted her chin. The spider lily moved with her swallow. "My father," she said. "When he drank, he lost the room. One night, when I was small, he held me under bathwater. I came out gasping. I used to hold that as proof I never mattered to him. Regression work brought me to the planning scene. Our souls sat together. He agreed to push me to the edge so I would claim my role in life. Now, that night marks a pivot. It wounded me and woke me."

The circle narrowed around her. Even breaths thickened.

"Thank you, Rowan," Hart said softly. "Extraordinary courage. What changed in how you hold him now?"

"I forgave him," she said. "He died last year in hospice. Before your work, I wished him dead every morning. After, I went to his bed. I held his hand. I told him we could dissolve the contract."

The man in the hoodie rubbed his face, palm rasping over stubble. "Mine's my son's killer," he said. "Drunk driver. I told you this already, Elian." His mouth twisted once before he steadied it. "Regression showed me my boy chose that exit. Our family needed a rupture to wake up. The driver's soul met ours before we came. They arranged the impact. I hated that man. Now I regard him as the one who carried the heavier role."

Headphones stopped twisting his bracelet while the man spoke. "Has this changed your grief?" Hart asked.

"Grief stays," Hoodie Man said. "Rage shifted. I stopped shaking my fist at the sky. I stopped asking what my son did to deserve it. I know now he volunteered."

Molly's nails pressed crescents into her palms. The quartz in her pocket pressed back, bone against stone.

The spider plant shed a brown leaf tip. It dropped onto the cabinet with a faint papery sound.

Hart switched off the flashlight. Darkness reclaimed his hand. "These stories show something essential," he said. "On the human layer, pain cuts deep. We validate it, we set boundaries, we pursue earthly justice where needed. On the soul layer, nothing unfolds without consent. No child enters a nightmare without first agreeing, with their team, to that pattern. Consciousness holds agency at every tier of reality."

Prior consent passed through the group like a coin rolled from palm to palm.

The tall person in the black sweater spoke without lifting her gaze. "A child with cancer," she said. "Hooked to chemo. The soul consented to that?"

"In many cases, yes," Hart answered. "Those souls often choose compressed paths—intense learning in brief spans. They can catalyze growth in families, medical systems, communities."

"And war?" She asked. "Whole villages burned?"

"Collective agreements," Hart said. "Group karma balancing, evolutionary movements on species level.

Immense pain, yes. Still held inside an intentional architecture."

The beads in Headphones' fingers resumed their circuit.

No child enters a nightmare without first agreeing returned in Molly's chest, now layered with another voice. Ren's voice in the valley: Do not hand what's yours away.

Rain tested the window glass with faster fingers.

Hart turned back to the board. Beneath the title, he wrote:

+ ACCELERATED GROWTH

+ KARMIC BALANCING

+ GAIA PARTICIPATION

"Sacred villains enter contracts for these reasons," he said. "They agree to absorb density, to catalyze awakening. On the surface screen, they enact cruelty. Behind it, souls honor their service."

Honor slid through Molly like a wrong key struck on a piano.

A moth brushed against one of the mandala lampshades. Wings tapped fabric, again and again. No opening offered, no route away from the light.

Brie drew her bag tighter. "My ex stalked me after I left," she said. "He wrapped his hands on my throat in a parking lot, thank goodness someone came along and he rushed off. His face is in my dreams. Therapy never touched it. Regression showed me his soul honoring our agreement to push me toward full departure. Once I understood, fear drained. I thanked his soul for keeping his promise."

Molly's voice moved before hesitation could stop it. "He had to place his hands on your throat to complete his side of a holy contract," she said. "Because without that, your soul misses a lesson."

Brie's gaze jerked up, then softened. "I had to reach that intensity," she said after a pause. "Otherwise, I might still be there."

"What about his responsibility now?" Molly asked. "Restraints, charges. Or does the contract cancel that ledger?"

Hart lifted his hand to steady the energy. "Important distinction," he said. "Soul-level collaboration never excuses human-level action. Contracts do not erase law. We can file reports, seek protection, imprison where necessary, while still holding the deeper frame. Meaning part of this agreement you made includes the earthly consequences."

"So on one level," Molly said, "he faces a judge. On another, he receives spiritual commendation for his performance."

A faint ripple crossed the circle. Hoodie Man shifted. Rowan reached for her own throat.

Hart met Molly's eyes. "The levels do not cancel each other," he said. "They run parallel. Our work invites you to hold both at once."

Headphones cleared his throat. "My sacred villain is me," he said. The words scraped the walls, cutting holes in the air's tension, releasing some of the pressure.

"I gambled away my little sister's college fund," he went on. "Our parents never recovered financially. My family fractured. Through regression, I saw our souls planning that fracture. I agreed to carry the betrayer role, to break patterns. She agreed to experience betrayal early and wake quicker than the rest. From that vantage, there's a strange…rightness."

"Do you plan to repair the loss? And what about your parents' roles in the agreement?" Molly asked.

His jaw tightened. "I'm trying," he said. "Working shifts, paying things down. My parents agreed to be the facilitators of my sister's and my agreement. It is honorable for them, I can see that now, so some of the guilt I had felt really lifted when I learned this."

Hart stepped in before tension sharpened. "Understanding the contract often ignites a desire to make amends," he said. "Awareness of soul agreements deepens responsibility; it never replaces it."

"Do you see clients whose guilt multiplies under this lens?" Molly asked quietly. "People already crushed under blame who hear they scripted the crush?"

"Not for me," Headphones explained. "I don't have guilt anymore, I feel as though I am a man of my word now, and look forward to learning more of my agreements."

"And your sister, your parents, do they feel fulfilment in their duties upholding the agreement?"

"In my experience," Hart cut in, "this framework lifts shame. Clients report relief. They exchange random punishment for chosen growth."

The spider plant leaned an arm of leaves on the wall. One tip brushed the whiteboard stand.

Molly sank back a little in her chair. The surrounding air thickened with lavender and damp clothing.

"Do you have an example," she asked, "of an extremely dark contract from your own practice? Not anger in a parking lot. Something that presses the limit."

Faces moved their glances toward him, searching not for spectacle but for permission to hold their own extremes.

Hart exhaled through his nose, expression shadowed by what he carried. "I'll alter details," he said. "What matters is the structure. A client came with complex trauma around childhood sexual abuse. Perpetrator: a trusted family friend, part of her spiritual community. Repeated violations, years of secrecy, grooming. She believed the universe neglected her. Progress with conventional therapy reached a plateau."

Did the spider plant just shake its head? Molly shook the notion out.

"In regression," he continued, "she encountered a pre-birth planning scene. Her soul and his sat in council. They agreed on a sequence designed to catalyze radical self-sovereignty. Her soul wished to move from dependency to unshakeable autonomy in this lifetime. His soul agreed to enact the violator role, with full knowledge of the human karma he would incur."

The air inside Molly's lungs went sharp and cold.

"She discovered what we call out-clause points," Hart said. "Moments where she could disclose, resist, seek help. As a child, she did not access them. As an adult, knowing those nodes existed shifted her narrative. She no longer held herself as a random victim in a godless world. She saw herself as co-author. That understanding changed everything."

"And the man?" Molly asked. Her voice felt like stone sliding over stone. "What did this understanding change for him? Was he thankful as a soul signing up for this? Is he proud of himself, here, after learning he played his part? Are there pedophiles planning this in the space between lives?"

Hart lifted his hands and lowered them. "His body died before our work together," he said. "Yet she encountered his soul in a between-lives setting. He wept. He expressed gratitude for her courage, remorse for the human damage, and was honored he could so this for her. She forgave him. Together they released the contract."

Tears gathered in Rowan's eyes, held at the brink. Brie pressed her lips together, knuckles whitening around her bag strap.

The moth struck the lampshade again and dropped to the rim, one wing clinging to the warm fabric, one hanging in thin air..

"You told her," Molly said, "that she agreed to her own rape? That she ordered it with her soul before she arrived?"

Hart rested his forearms on his knees, fingers loosely interlaced. His voice remained even.

"I walked with her while she discovered that truth," he replied. "I did not impose it. Her own higher-self confirmed it. The effect on her life was liberating."

"You framed the abuse as a lesson she requested," Molly said. "The man became a soul who loved her enough to enact horror."

"On the soul plane, yes," Hart said. "On Earth, his actions remain indefensible. Both truths stand, however offensive that might sound to certain parts of the psyche."

She studied him. "Do you hear how that sounds?" she asked. "Outside of this room?"

He inclined his head slightly. "To a mind that knows only the Earth level, it can sound brutal," he said. "But tell me, Molly—what is the alternative you prefer? That she was a random target in a meaningless universe? That there was no structure, no context, only cruelty?"

"I prefer reality," she said. "Even if it is unstructured."

"And what if reality is structured whether we like it or not?" he asked. "If pattern exists, would denying it serve her? Or you?"

Her hand tightened in her lap.

"She could believe," he continued, "that she was pure victim, that nothing in her had any say at any level. How does that belief tend to play out over a lifetime? You have seen it. Freeze. Hypervigilance. A constant sense that the next blow may come from anywhere, for no reason."

"That does happen," Molly said. "Because someone hurt her. Not because she misread cosmic paperwork."

"Of course," Hart said. "And yet, when she saw that her soul had chosen to use that man's darkness as a catalyst, something changed. She stopped asking, 'Why me?' and started asking, 'What can I do with this?' Is that not a meaningful shift?"

"It is a shift," she said. "It does not prove the premise."

He let the words hang, then asked quietly, "Have you never noticed that you feel calmer when there is at least a frame around what happened to you?"

She hesitated. "Sometimes," she admitted.

"Exactly," Hart said. "The nervous system settles when chaos becomes comprehensible. Now, ask yourself: is it kinder to tell your body, 'This was pointless,' or, 'I chose, at a level deeper than memory, to face this and transform it'?"

"It feels kinder to say I chose it," she said slowly. "And

also like a betrayal of myself."

"Of which self?" he asked. "The frightened you here? Or the larger self that knew her own strength before she ever arrived?"

Molly looked away, toward the window, where the frosted glass turned the city into a smear of light.

"What if the frightened me is the only self that matters here?" she said.

"In legal terms, yes," Hart said. "In psychological terms, absolutely. We must honour her. But in spiritual terms, there is more of you than that girl. Are you willing to consider that both levels deserve a voice?"

She did not answer.

He softened his tone further.

"When you resist this idea," he said, "what part of you speaks? Is it the part that longs to stay in control by believing you were only acted upon? Or is it the part that is afraid that if you admit any agency, you will be blamed?"

"I am afraid of being blamed," she said. "Because people already blame victims without soul contracts."

"And I do not blame you," Hart said. "I blame no one at the soul level. I only ask: which interpretation leads you toward power, and which leaves you in permanent reaction to one man's choices?"

Molly's throat tightened. "Power at the price of truth is not worth much," she said.

"Agreed," he said at once. "So let us look at what recurs across hundreds of regressions. When clients go deep enough, unprompted, they describe planning rooms, councils, agreements. They speak the same phrases. Does it not at least merit consideration? Or do we dismiss all of them to protect one part of your mind from discomfort?"

"Are you saying my discomfort is the problem?" she asked.

"I am saying your discomfort is understandable,"

he replied. "And that it may not be the best guide. Trauma always protests when old meaning structures dissolve. The ego hears, 'You chose this,' and translates it as, 'You are to blame.' But that is not what the soul hears."

"And you know what my soul hears better than I do?" Defiance claimed her voice.

He held her gaze with a steady calm.

"I know what souls tend to show, when the conscious mind steps aside," he said. "You came here because the explanations you have tried so far have not relieved you. Is that fair?"

She exhaled. "Yes," she said. "That is fair."

"Then allow yourself to ask," Hart said gently, "whether your resistance protects you, or whether it keeps you circling the same pain. If your higher self showed you, without my words, that you chose certain themes, would you want to know? Or would you prefer to maintain a position that leaves you permanently at the mercy of others' choices?"

"That is not a simple question," she said.

"I do not expect a simple answer," he replied. "I only ask you to notice the choice. You can cling to a narrative in which you were written upon and never holding the pen, or you can test a narrative in which, somewhere beyond memory, you lifted the pen first."

Molly sat very still.

He let a few seconds pass, then added, "You do not have to agree with me now. You do not have to agree with me ever. But if you close the door on this framework without examining it, are you certain you are choosing freely? Or are you reacting against the idea because a younger part of you fears being misunderstood?"

The question slid under her skin with uncomfortable precision. She felt the familiar urge to defend, and underneath it, the quieter urge to be done with defending anything at all.

"I do not know," she said.

"That," Hart said softly, "is an honest place to begin. From there, we explore. Not to erase your truth, but to expand it."

He sat back, giving her space.

"If you decide," he added, "that even after seeing everything, you still cannot accept the notion of prior agreements, I will respect that. But let us reach that conclusion from knowledge, not from fear of what it might mean."

The spider plant surrendered another leaf. It tore away near the base and fell to the carpet between Molly's shoes.

No one's gaze moved down.

"Something in me resists that," Molly said. "Not from a place of outrage for its own sake. From a place that remembers that child's body could never sign anything."

"The personality did not sign," Hart said. "The soul did. Infant bodies, sick bodies, even those in comas carry soul-level agreements. That is the point. Choice transcends what the mind recognizes as consent."

Buzz Cut whispered, "It feels heavy and beautiful," and wiped her cheek with the heel of her hand.

Hoodie Man nodded once, as though some puzzle in him clicked.

Inside Molly, a different structure locked into place: If a God endorsed contracts of that kind, perhaps that God isn't what we think.

In the river valley, Ren knelt again on the flat stone, fingers trailing water. Bark on the nearest trunk rearranged itself. The word NO grew thicker, darker, more carved.

Hart capped his marker. "The mind often pushes against these ideas," he said. "Ego prefers linear justice. I invite you to listen with the heart. Ask: Does the heart expand at the idea that no pain touches you without your prior consent? That your soul remains sovereign even inside your worst memories?"

Palms lifted to chests. Nods moved through the circle.

Molly's hand closed around the quartz. CLARITY pressed a clean crescent into her skin.

"Homework for the week," Hart said. "Journal about your sacred villain. Write a letter from your soul to theirs. Acknowledge the contract. Allow gratitude or rage. Either holds power. Bring what arises into future work."

Pens began to move. Headphones bent over his notebook. Brie wrote quickly. Rowan watched ink gather at the tip of her pen without touching paper.

The moth had stopped fighting. One wing stuck to the lampshade, translucence lit from behind. Light burned through a thin triangle of membrane.

Hart closed the evening with a brief blessing. "May you honor the bravery of every soul who challenges you. May you recognize love under every dark mask. May your contracts complete with grace."

Chairs groaned as people rose. Hugs passed from body to body, soft words of support traded, numbers ex-changed. The room began to loosen.

Molly stayed seated until the doorway thinned. Hoodie Man gave her shoulder a companionable squeeze as he passed. "You ask sharp questions," he said. "That means you're getting closer to peace."

"Peace with what?" she asked.

"With all of it," he said, and moved on.

Hart approached, he placed his hands on her shoulders and looked her in the eyes. "Your strong reactions today signal a close proximity to a core agreement," he said. "Your questions carried a particular heat and paired with anger can mark a threshold."

"What waits on the other side?" she asked.

"Acceptance," he said dropping his hands. "Of the architecture. Once you grasp that you chose even the darkest corridors, something heavier than anger drops away."

Lightning flared outside; the brief white flash doubled his reflection in the window. Two Elians overlapped, both with the same earnest gaze.

"Or," she said.

"If this frame harms more than it heals, we adjust," he said. "My sense, though? Your soul stood behind you when you pressed me tonight. That same soul brought you here because you hover at the edge of remembering an important contract tied to your childhood. Tied to that door."

The internal image of the swollen wood flickered at the edge of her awareness. So did the blurred figure in the valley, the one Ren barred her from crossing.

"Maybe my soul dragged me here to put God on the stand," she said quietly.

His mouth curved. "Good," he said. "Deity withstands cross-examination. See you in session, Molly. Sleep with intention tonight."

She stepped out into the hallway. The office goldfish

swam its tireless loop, turning the same corner of glass again and again. Near the entrance, automatic doors exhaled cold air at her as she passed.

Outside, the rain had thinned to drizzle. Puddles held fractured reflections of streetlamps, yellow halos rip-pling each time a drop struck.

On the walk home, the city carried on: sirens slicing the distance, laughter spilling from a bar patio, a dog barking at something behind a fence. A train horn cut across it all, mournful and long.

At one corner, a man with a bent shopping cart shouted toward the clouded sky. "You wrote it!" he yelled. "You signed it! Don't throw this at me!" His voice cracked on the last word.

A woman with a grocery bag adjusted her grip and crossed the street without altering pace.

Wind shoved damp air into Molly's coat. The stone in her pocket dragged along her thigh with each stride.

CLARITY. CLARITY. CLARITY.

In the river place, water continued its course with no paper tacked to its surface, no clauses in its flow. Ren trailed his hand, reading currents. The nearest tree thickened its bark into that single, blunt word.

NO.

Back in her apartment, she dropped the quartz onto the kitchen counter. It landed beside her mother's latest offering—a magnet stuck to the fridge that read: You Chose This Life For A Reason.

She peeled the magnet away and placed it face-down.

Outside, rain gathered strength again. It hammered roofs and glass and branches, obeying gradients of heat and pressure and its old arrangement with gravity—an agreement of its own.

Chapter Five

The Memory Door

Night pressed fingers along Molly's throat and kept them there.

Sleep arrived in thin slabs that cracked under thought. Each descent fractured. Each rise dragged pieces of the day with it—Rowan in bathwater, Brie against a car, Hoodie Man on the highway shoulder, Hart's hands shaping the air while he spoke of sacred villains.

On the third attempt, exhaustion gained ground.

Darkness gathered and thickened. Walls assembled around her. A corridor stretched ahead, narrow and long, lined on both sides with doors that rose from floor to a ceiling lost in shadow. Brass plates hung where peepholes might have gone.

YOU ASKED FOR THIS. YOU AGREED.

YOU KNEW.

The letters stood cleanly incised. No handles interrupted the wood. No locks guarded anything. Only smooth panels and the phrases.

A voice spoke from the corridor itself, from floor and ceiling at once. Calm, measured, the kind of tone designed to bypass defenses.

"You drafted these," it said. "You signed. You insisted."

Ink began to bleed from the engraved lines. Black drops formed, fat and slow, then slid downward. Puddles spread across the floor and inched toward her bare toes with the focus of oil.

Her hand rose toward the nearest door. Wood under her palm ran cold, grain raised like goose-flesh. Another sentence pressed up from the far side, backwards against the panel. Only skin read it.

YOU COULD HAVE LEFT.

Heat pushed out from the walls. Air thickened with the scent of old incense and damp plaster.

The goldfish from Hart's waiting room glided past her shins, bowl and all, glass moving through the ink without leaving a wake. Its mouth opened and closed. Each gape released a new string of words that drifted upward, adhered to the ceiling, and remained there.

NO VICTIMS.

ONLY AGREEMENTS.

The corridor shuddered from end to end.

Her heart hammered. Fabric tugged at her thigh. The stone that followed her even here pressed its word against her skin.

CLARITY.

A second voice threaded through the first. Thinner,

yet steadier. Wire through rope.

Do not accept contracts written invisibly with your blood. Ren.

The brass plates wavered. Letters smeared, then ran, black streaks slid into one another until words lost shape. The doors blurred. The corridor widened and thinned and dissolved into a flat gray field.

Her alarm tore through at six-twenty.

Her hand slapped the phone. Silence dropped. Sheets clung to her back. Sweat cooled along her spine in a narrow strip. Outside, traffic already moved; a bus sighed past, brakes exhaling metal fatigue.

Her hair tangled against the pillowcase, strands carrying a faint ghost of lavender from the diffuser she had abandoned a few weeks earlier. When she shifted, something hard pressed under the other pillow. Fingers closed around the quartz. The stone lay there as if it had slept beside her. She carried no memory of putting it there.

The windows shone, washed clear by the night's rain. The cloud cover had pulled back from the edges of the city, where light waited.

Molly's phone pulsed with a reminder. Regression – 1:00 p.m.

She stared until the letters blurred, then set the device on the nightstand. "Of course, today," she said into the room.

No answer came from the drywall, or the radiator.

Hart greeted her with his usual warm half bow. "Come in," he said. "Your color runs a little thin. How has the week moved through you?"

The office plants had reached farther since last time. The fern near the window had pushed two new shoots toward the recliner, tips pointed like green antennae.

Molly lowered herself into the armchair. "Intense dreams," she said. "Hallway of doors with slogans carved into them. No handles. Ink. And, your goldfish swam through the mess."

Interest sharpened the lines around Hart's eyes. "Text on the doors?" he asked.

"Choice rhetoric," she said. "You asked for this, you agreed, you knew."

He sat and uncapped his pen. "Symbols from my space often appear," he said. "The psyche borrows what lies near to build metaphors. Goldfish, doors. How did you engage with them?"

"I put a hand on one," she said. "The other side pressed back. It accused me of staying."

He nodded. "The mind protests any frame that redirects responsibility inward," he said. "Especially when blame has long pointed outward. We will be careful."

"Your emails promise accelerated growth," she said. "Careful rarely appears on the flyer."

"I might amend the flyers then." A faint smile flickered, then faded. He studied her face for a long breath. "Your Ren will probably bring us closer to your core agreement today," he said. "My sense is a childhood scene waits behind that memory door we touched. Do you trust yourself to approach it?"

Trust. The word sent a thread of red through her chest.

"I trust my ability to stop," she said.

"Good. Nice healthy boundary," he said. "Let's honor that." He rolled the recliner into place. "Same descent. Breath, valley, guide. The unconscious likes familiar routes."

She stretched out. The cushion cupped her weight. Ferntips hovered at the edge of her vision, shadows against glass.

Hart's voice gentled, dropping into the practiced cadence that soothed other people's nervous systems. "Inhale. Long. Exhale longer. Let the body sink. Count yourself down the stairs—ten to one. With each number, more weight drains from your limbs."

The inner staircase appeared on cue. Her bare feet

met each step. No splinter. No misplacement. The grooves cut into the treads ran deeper now, as though she had walked this way many times.

At the bottom waited the door: same wood, same crossbar, same thin seam of light along the floor.

"Open it when you're ready," Hart said.

Her palm met the panel. A pulse answered. A living beat under her hand.

Ren's remembered words curved through the air: This door requires no contract. You chose this path before language.

Her fingers pressed.

The valley rose around her in one sweep. River, low hills, trees whose bark carried script, grass brushing her shins. Light poured from no discernible sun, yet everything carried a clear outline. A bird with turquoise feathers perched on a stone near the water. It regarded her with one dark eye, then launched. A single down feather remained on the rock, quivering.

Ren stood partway up the path, already waiting. Their features shifted between ages again, anchored only by the stone-gray steadiness of their gaze. Edges around their mouth held more strain today.

"Welcome Back," they said. "Come explore."

"Good afternoon to you as well," she said.

Hart's voice floated in from the outer room, thinner here but still distinct. "Greet Ren," he prompted. "Invite him to show you a formative scene connected to this lifetime's core contract. A primary challenge. Guides know where to take you."

Cold drew along her arms despite the valley warmth. Air altered, as though an unseen cloud slid across what-ever passed for a sun in this place.

"Your therapist pushes for contract imagery," Ren said. "His intent grows from care; his map still carries fractures. Brace yourself."

"Tell him that," she said.

"He hears only you," Ren replied. "Not us."
82

A narrower path appeared, cutting away from the river and up between trees. Shade gathered thick along it. The bark-script on these trunks bit deeper, as if words had been carved by something with less patience.

Ren gestured. "Up," he said. "We meet a door you nailed shut with your own hands."

They climbed. Grass gave way to ground packed hard and dry, laced with roots like knuckles under skin. Sensation increased without fatigue—pressure in calves, a tug behind knees, lungs pulling in air that thinned with every step.

Halfway, the scent around them shifted. Pine and clean water receded. Another smell bled through— cheap sandalwood incense, sharp and chemical, layered over sweat and floor cleaner.

A rectangle of light formed on the slope ahead. Eight feet high, three wide. Free-standing at first, a sheer panel against the air.

As they drew closer, the glow dimmed and revealed

wood beneath. Yellow paint. A long scar near the bottom where some heavy thing had once scraped it.

Her skin prickled in a wave from scalp to ankle. Her breath shortened in two hard pulls.

"This one opens from both sides," Ren said.

Hart: "Stand before the doorway. Remember, you control depth of immersion. You can watch from across the room or through your own eyes."

Ren's fingers brushed hers. "I will stay with you," they said. "No replay without a witness."

A child's voice rose inside her chest, the pitch identical to the one that used to call across apartment courtyards. I don't want to.

Ren's grip strengthened. "I know," they said. "But, the part that booked this session answered differently. She brought your older self here to hold the door while she shakes."

Heat seeped through the yellow paint. Voices leaked under the threshold—one lower register, smooth and measured; high chiming sounds around it, like re-corded bells.

"Your choice," Ren said.

Her hand rose. Fingers closed around the knob. Met-al chilled the skin along her palm. Memory of pres-sure flooded through: the slight resistance, the roll, the soft click of the latch.

She turned.

Light stepped through.

Incense crowded her throat. A brass burner shaped like a lotus smoked on a low table, petals blackened along their tips. Smoke coiled upward in tight ropes.

Posters covered the walls. A goddess stood on a prone body, tongue red, eyes wide and crimson. A robed shepherd carried a lamb. A many-armed figure brandished weapons and blossoms. Plastic lamina-tion lent their faces an oiled sheen.

Twelve-year-old Molly sat cross-legged on a sun-pat-terned yoga mat, spine pressed against the edge of the bed. Her hands rested on her knees because he had told her that stance anchored energy. Her T-shirt clung to her back. Seams scratched skin at her shoulders.

Across from her, he knelt on his own mat. Linen pants, bare feet, palms sliding beads along a string. A strand of hair slipped free from the knot at his neck. His voice hummed through the smoke in a soothing drone.

"Breathe," he said. "Deep into the belly. You move with water. Old soul."

Adult Molly stood in the doorway with Ren, heart pounding against bone. The room ignored them. This version of him lived inside its sealed loop.

Hart's voice drifted around the edges. "Notice the dynamic," he said. "Teacher, student. Spiritual language."

Twelve pressed her nails into her knees until crescents reddened skin. Her eyes shone from incense. A twitch at her mouth betrayed some internal recoil.

"You carry advanced contracts," the man said. "Not everyone signs on for this depth. Many souls choose ease. You chose challenge. Brave."

Beads clicked under his fingers, small wooden impacts that measured time more accurately than any clock.

"Old soul," he repeated. "You remember that you chose me as your teacher, yes?"

Twelve's throat bobbed. "My mom says that," she answered. "That I chose her. And you."

"Your mother perceives well." He smiled, slow and sure. "She recognized our agreement. You and I sat together between lives. We designed a path. You remember?"

No images reached her yet his tone painted them anyway: clouds bright as paper lanterns, scrolls, signatures. Her own small luminous self nodding solemnly across a table.

"You knew your childhood was needed, we all have

lessons, and others help us achieve those lessons." he continued. "Hardship squeezes gifts out of hiding. You asked for help with that. You chose me." His eyes stayed on her face. The beads kept sliding.

Ren murmured near Molly's ear. "Hear it," he said. "Exact vocabulary. Contract. Choice. Agreement."

"Remember," the man said, "on the soul level you remain safe. No matter what arises here. Your higher-self led you. Agreed, little one?"

Twelve nodded. "Agreed," she echoed.

Ren: "Echoing, is not consent."

Heat pooled again, heavier. Sweat crept from the small of Twelve's back up into her hairline.

"Today," he said, "we support the solar plexus. Third chakra. Seat of power."

The word power hung in the air without landing anywhere in the room.

He shifted closer. The beads stilled. His hands extended over her midsection, hovering.

"May I place my hands here for alignment?" he asked. "Touch enhances the work."

Her pulse stuttered at her throat.

He had taught lessons on boundaries. Spiritual integrity. Consent as sacred. He had praised her when she agreed to breathing exercises, to visualization, to chanting.

In the valley, water snarled around unseen rocks.

Hart's whisper threaded back in: "Watch her body. Posture, movement, sensation."

Twelve's shoulders rounded. Knees drew fractionally together. Fingers scraped cloth, small claws.

"You trust me," he said. No question.

Earlier in this same room, she had told him I trust you, voice full of fierce adolescent loyalty. That declaration now pressed on her chest like a weight.

She dipped her head.

"Good," he said. "Trust amplifies our work."

His hands lowered until his palms lay against her T-shirt, fingers spread across her abdomen.

Cold shot through her. Her body shrank away in tiny, invisible increments.

Adult Molly's stomach clenched in sympathetic echo. Nails dug deeper into her own palms. Fabric from Hart's blanket rasped her skin.

"You might experience discomfort," the man said. "Energy moving. Old pain rising from cells. Remember: your soul chose this. There are no accidents."

His left hand slid lower, heel pressing against the waistband.

The goddess on the poster gazed down, eyes wide, tongue extended. The salt lamp on the dresser brightened to a fierce orange. Smoke curved around his head, drawing a thin, brittle halo.

"Breathe through it," he murmured. "Some part resists; that part carries fear. Your soul wants this. Your mind protests."

My soul wants this. My mind protests. The phrases folded into her.

Hart's present voice brushed the frame. "You observe a distorted expression of a sacred principle," he said softly. "The teacher is misusing cosmic truth. Note where responsibility lies."

Ren stepped close to the scene and pressed his palm against unseen glass. Fingertips meeting resistance. The room continued unchanged, sealed by time's first decision.

"Ask your soul," the man said, "why you chose this contact. What lesson arises through this sacred touch."

Twelve scrambled for correct answers. I chose to learn trust. I chose to surrender. I chose to master boundaries. Every possibility led back to him.

Her body delivered a different scripture: muscles tightening, skin crawling, a weight of nausea at the base of her tongue. Doctrine raced ahead of sensation and named those responses ego.

"If something inside resists," he had told her last week, "that often signals ego fear. Remember your soul wants this, but your ego clings to comfort."

Sacred villain. Tough love. The integration circle's language marched into this room and took seats.

Adult Molly's breath rasped. The recliner's fabric pressed against her back. The office's faint lamp hum wove through.

"This touches the core," Hart murmured from nearby. "You encounter the human role-player behind a difficult agreement. Stay anchored in the chair. You can step back whenever you choose."

Another touch sounded, from outside the vision. A smack against glass. Something dark struck Hart's window, wings outstretched, feathers splaying. A crow fought gravity for one shuddering heartbeat and clawed its way back into the sky. One feather clung to the wet pane, then slid away.

Hart's attention flicked to the window, then back. "You're safe here," he said. "He cannot enter this room."

Words reached her through cotton.

"He used your language," Molly said, voice rough, eyes closed against the light. "Soul-level love. Agreements. Depth."

Hart's pen hovered above the page, a slim metal dragonfly stalled in midair.

"Spiritual truths echo across lineages," he said. "Counterfeits imitate them. He misapplied a real concept. The contract remains; his human expression violated it."

The fern beside the bookshelf held its breath. Each leaf leaned toward her, green ears, green tongues.

"So," Hart continued, softer, "your soul may have chosen this distorted teacher to learn discernment.

Or, Molly, you stood there as his teacher. You have a strong soul constitution; you could have agreed to be the child for him to learn from."

Heat slid through her chest, down into her gut, thick as tar. The couch fabric rasped along her palms; fibers scratched at her skin, warning or accusation.

Her eyes snapped open.

Ceiling tiles stared back, flat and blank. Sweat cooled along her temples. The fern's leaves drooped again, each central vein pulsing like a thin green artery.

"A teacher," she said. The word scraped her tongue on the way out. "Me?"

Hart nodded once. Lines deepened between his brows, a solemn furrow carved for her benefit.

"Teachers of light often carry the heaviest contracts," he said. "Children with advanced souls incarnate into dense patterns. They volunteer for families where the curriculum stretches them."

Curriculum. The word pressed against her teeth.

Classrooms swam up: chalk dust, plastic chairs, the sharp click of doors. A different door, a different room: breath that smelled of coffee and mint gum; wallpaper moons fading behind a man's shoulders.

Her throat closed.

"He said I invited his hands," she whispered. "He told me that. That I brought it in." The upholstery under her fingers buckled, as if the couch recoiled from the sentence.

Hart's gaze rested on her face, steady, unblinking. The room's air tilted toward him, as if the vents exhaled for his lungs alone.

"And that…" Her voice turned brittle. "That tracks with this? With what you say? Contracts. Volunteering."

"It echoes a truth while twisting it," Hart said. "On the human level, you did not consent. A child cannot consent. His behavior broke every ethical earth boundary."

The clock on the shelf ticked on, but each tick landed inside her ribs, not on the wall.

"At the soul level," Hart went on, "another layer operates. A broader choreography. Souls agree to roles that look brutal from inside our lives here. That does not excuse the human crime. It offers you a path to reclaim meaning and power, instead of remaining frozen as a passive victim."

Passive victim. The words latched onto her. Hooks in tender flesh. A shame flushed hot beneath her skin.

"I don't know how to hold both," she murmured. "Victim and… volunteer." The last word tasted poisonous. Her tongue pressed against her teeth, as if it tried to push the syllables back.

"You hold both by widening your vantage," Hart said. "From the ground, a storm feels cruel. From above, it irrigates a valley. Your soul selected an intense syllabus. That points to courage, not defect."

The fern trembled, a faint rattle of leaves that reached the air before it reached her ears. The plant leaned away from the window, toward the door, toward escape.

Her body thrummed with dissonance, strings tuned by two hands at once. One hand belonged to a man in a dim room with locked blinds. The other sat across from her now, blue ink ready to convert her story into neat syllables.

"If my soul chose it," she said slowly, "does that… lessen what he did?"

"No." Hart's reply came swift, trimmed, professional. "At the human level, his choice generated karma, consequence, responsibility. Legal, ethical, energetic. That ledger stands. At the soul level, love includes severe teachers and sometimes even more severe students. Tough love enters as trauma, illness, loss. From the highest vantage, you may have volunteered for a heavy role in your evolution. You can still fulfill yours on earth through forgiveness."

"By forgiving?" The word sagged on her tongue.

"By recognizing your magnitude," Hart said. "By

stepping out of a flat narrative where you exist only as a harmed child. By owning that your essence never touched his hands, that your soul orchestrated growth even inside violation. That restores agency."

Agency. The syllables rang hollow, like coins dropped into a well without bottom.

Her stomach clenched. A faint nausea crawled upward, algae in sluggish water. The couch's seams dug into her thighs, tiny ridges that spelled out a code her skin could not read.

"What if I miss the lesson?" she asked. "If I fail the... curriculum."

Hart's smile tilted, sorrowful and proud at once. "You cannot fail," he said. "Curriculum adapts. Lifetimes recur. In one, you stay small and frightened. In another, you expand into a healer, a guide. From the larger perspective, all threads serve learning."

All threads. The phrase wrapped around her wrists. Every path bent toward the same altar. No exit, only interpretation.

Hart set the pen on the side table. Metal kissed wood with a tiny decisive click.

"For now," he said, "let this idea sit in the field. No need to force integration. Your body will digest at its own pace. Notice where constriction softens over the next days. That will signal alignment."

The fern drooped farther, leaves brushing the floor, as if it tried to hide its roots.

Molly nodded because her neck moved on its own. Paper rustled as Hart closed his notebook. The room folded itself back into neutrality: chair, couch, fern, clock, bookshelf. A set. A stage awaiting the next scene.

"Take care, Molly," he said.

In the waiting room, the goldfish traced its usual oval, fins fanning. The framed print above the chairs still showed the oak with its rope swing. The hand-lettered line beneath had shifted inside its glass.

You chose this playground now read: You chose this

ground.

Outside, the afternoon opened in sharp light. Clouds had torn. Sun struck the sidewalk in hard white slabs. Shadows cut cleaner lines along parked cars and tree trunks.

* * *

At home, steam coated the bathroom mirror, a dense white veil over her reflection. Water thundered from the showerhead, each drop a hard coin striking tile. The drain gurgled, eager, greedy.

Molly stepped under the spray. Heat lashed her shoulders, scalded a path down her back. Soap slid across her skin in frantic strokes. Lather foamed over arms, breasts, stomach, thighs. Her palms scrubbed until the skin flushed raw, until red patches bloomed like warning lights across her body.

He misapplied a real concept.

Your soul may have chosen this distorted teacher.

You could have agreed to be the child to help him learn.

Hart's phrases clung thicker than the steam. Syllables seeped into collarbones, lodged in the hollow of her throat. They crowded the tender skin behind her knees, the inside of her wrists, the scarred corridors of childhood.

Water hammered harder, as if the pipes pushed it with anger. Droplets ricocheted, united, slid in currents that traced the path of old hands. Along her ribs. Across her hips. Between her thighs.

A shiver climbed her spine. Muscles braced against memory and theory at once. The shower walls pressed inward, tile squares leaning closer, eager to hear which story she would choose.

"Victim," she whispered. The word barely cleared her lips before the spray crushed it. "Volunteer." That one came out sharper, a shard that cut her tongue.

Steam thickened around her, an unseen auditorium. The water carried both words down her skin, past her knees, into the drain, yet no relief rose to replace them. The soap's perfume—citrus and pine—fought the ghost of old cologne, stale coffee breath, Hart's sandalwood office.

Her nails dragged over her arms again, deeper this time. Red crescents lined the scrubbed skin. The water refused to cool; heat pinned her in place, a liquid hand against her back.

You may have volunteered for a heavy role.

You cannot fail the curriculum.

The phrases braided with older commands from another mouth. You wanted this. You brought me in. You're special.

Words turned viscous, a film across her body. Each sentence from each man fused into a glaze the water could not lift.

The showerhead rattled, metal throat protesting. A single drop landed in the cup of her ear, a hot whisper with no language.

Molly pressed her forehead to the tile. Cold seeped from the ceramic into her skin, a thin relief, sharp and honest. The grout lines radiated outward from her brow like chalk marks on a crime scene floor.

"Wash off," she rasped. "Wash off."

The water surged. It beat down in fierce solidarity, yet Hart's vocabulary stayed pressed against her, a second skin under the first. The idea of volunteer, of teacher, burrowed deeper, crawling beneath the red scrubbed surface, seeking bone.

Outside the curtain, the bathroom light flickered. Bulb and switch conferred in faint clicks. The mirror's fog swirled, as if a breath traced words on the glass and erased them before they formed.

Inside the stall, soap, water, tile, and steam labored over her body, loyal and relentless. His touch no longer haunted her skin; his doctrine did.

Chapter Six

Split Screen

Morning opened with the kettle's hiss and a wall of slogans.

Hairline cracks branched from the kitchen ceiling, fine as veins. Below them, her mother's magnets clung to the fridge in a dense cluster of gloss and insistence:

You chose this family

Earth School: Tough Curriculum, Great Re-wards Your Soul Said YES

The newest magnet lay face-down on the counter. Condensation from last night had dried around it in a faint ring, as if the object had sweated through its own message.

Her phone vibrated against the table. Mom.

She let it hum through three pulses, then brought it to her ear.

"Morning, star child." Pots shifted in the background; something metal knocked ceramic. "I woke at 3:33 thinking about you. Angel number. How did it go with Elian?"

Steam built inside the kettle. "We reached a memory," Molly said. "The room. Him. Incense. Beads. Your old friend from the apartment."

The clatter on the other end dulled. Air between them thinned. "Ah," her mother said at last. "He surfaced."

"The regression dropped me straight onto that mat," Molly said. "He framed things the way Hart does. Contracts. Old soul. Agreement. Same vocabulary, different incense burner."

Her mother exhaled a long thread of breath. "Sweetheart," she said, voice low now. "You know he twisted sacred teachings. That's why his life shredded. Elian's the opposite. He untangles what that man knotted. You need that."

"I remember what you told me after I told you what happened," Molly said. "You lit a candle. You took my hands. You said we'd all agreed to this lesson as a family."

On her mother's side, a cupboard door eased shut. "I reached for the only frame that stopped me from falling apart," she said. "If your soul chose it, then it wasn't meaningless cruelty. That thought let me keep breathing."

"So, my body protected your theology," Molly said.

"That's not fair," her mother replied sharply. "I was drowning. The contracts showed me a raft. They still do. If we wrote this together before birth, we're not victims. We're brave."

The magnet on the counter caught a strand of sunlight. The gloss revealed its buried line for an instant:

You Chose This Life For A Reason.

"I want a world where his decision stays on his shoulders," Molly said. "Not spread over mine in the name of bravery."

"This doesn't come from blame," her mother said. "It comes from soul. Souls don't think in 'fault.' They move in evolution, in balance. When I sat with my guide about your birth, she showed me the contract. You chose a hard path to wake others, including me. The abuse arrived inside that agreement. I still hate it here"—a pan scraped somewhere—"but on the higher level, love lives there."

"Love," Molly repeated. The word settled like smoke that refused to thin.

"For your courage," her mother said. "For what you volunteered to carry. You came as a teacher. You've always known that."

"I teach user flows," Molly said. "Logins, checkout carts. That's enough curriculum."

"You armor yourself with this humor," her mother answered. "It keeps grace from landing. Stay with Elian. Let him guide you instead of litigating everything. Victim ideals grips tight. Contracts loosen it."

"If healing demands I thank the man who hurt me," Molly said quietly, "I prefer the wound."

The kettle clicked off. Steam curled, white against the dull kitchen paint.

"Those are words from pain, not from your higher self," her mother said. "I'll light a candle. Ask your team to reach you in dreams. They're sending signs—you keep missing them."

"Crows hitting windows?" Molly asked. "Heard them loud and clear."

"Crows bring messages," her mother said. "Death and rebirth. They're auspicious. I'll send you a link."

"Don't," Molly said.

"I love you," her mother murmured. "On every level."

"On this one," Molly replied. "That's enough," and ended the call before silence forced either of them to choose a softer line.

Placing the phone in her bag, she headed out. The grocery store hummed under fluorescent lights. Refrigeration units droned at the edges. Mist hissed over the produce, coating the kale and lettuce in tiny beads that caught the overhead glare.

Molly guided the cart with a narrow focus. Coffee. Yogurt. Eggs. Bread. Her list anchored her to shelves, to UPC codes, to the small certainty of barcodes and prices.

Near an endcap of canned tomatoes, a thought tapped her shoulder. Not sound. Not scent. The feel of the air.

She turned her head and met herself in the glass of the fire extinguisher case.

Same coat. Same hair. Same tired set to the jaw. But the other Molly's shoulders lay looser, mouth softened at the corners. A child's hand clasped her sleeve—small fingers in pink mittens, curls caught in a lopsided ponytail. They leaned together over a jar, a shopping list tucked under the child's arm in messy crayon handwriting.

The other Molly bent and pressed a kiss to that small crown, entirely present.

No phone. No invisible corridor of doors.

Molly blinked. Red metal stared back. Hose. Gauge. Inspection tag yellowed at the edges.

Her grip on the cart tightened. The metal frame shuddered.

In the freezer aisle, the glass held a different version. Hospital bracelet peeking from under a cuff. Hair thinner. Left sleeve hanging loose, pinned where bone should continue. The reflected Molly met her gaze, then lifted what remained of her forearm in a brief, rueful greeting.

Behind the glass, stacked frozen dinners glowed under blue light.

She shut the freezer door harder than necessary. Cold fogged then cleared.

Two aisles later, by paper towels, the convex mirror in the corner caught the whole row. It warped shoppers into small planets, each orbiting a separate gravity.

Inside that curvature, she saw herself three times: pushing a stroller; moving slowly with a cane; walking in prison orange, wrists bare, no bracelets, expression flat.

The angles slid across one another as she moved, then scattered.

Laughter echoed from the next aisle—a father coaxing a toddler into choosing cereal. The ordinary intimacy of it cut cleaner than any image.

She parked the cart beside a display of discounted candles and leaned on the handle until the plastic bit her palms.

Parallel lives had lived in her reading list for years— articles, diagrams, threads. Here, under the supermarket's fluorescent sky, they pressed against the glass.

If every fork in the path exists somewhere, who exactly drafts contracts?

Who sits in a council room planning suffering when an uncountable number of branches could already carry every configuration of it?

A different cart clipped her ankle. "Sorry," someone muttered, already moving past.

She forced herself through self-checkout. The scanner's voice chirped instructions, indifferent to the weight in her chest. Credit card. Receipt. Bags.

Outside, wind shoved at her, sharp and damp. One handle stretched white along the plastic, threatening to tear. She adjusted her grip to head home.

A bus glided past, windows shining dull.

For a moment, the glass showed another pair of figures walking where she walked—her and a man beside her. His profile tugged at recognition: the

112

abuser's mouth without its slyness, the eyes without their appraisal. Two adults, hands interlaced, no incense, no mat.

The bus turned the corner and took them away.

By the time she reached her building, muscles between her shoulder blades burned.

Lena lay stretched along her couch like a thrown coat, socks misaligned, mug cupped between her palms. She had texted: inside. using the key, don't scream—before letting herself in.

Molly dropped the grocery bags on the counter. One apple rolled free, bumped against a cabinet, and settled.

"Do you ever see…other versions of yourself ?" she asked.

Lena peered over the mug. "In photographs, sure. Those bangs were a crime."

"In glass," Molly said. "Windows. Security mirrors. For a second, they move differently. They're with people who aren't here. Or missing parts I still have."

Lena straightened a little. "Did you see this, Today?"

"Yeah, At the grocery store," Molly said. "One with a child. One with a hospital band and no left fore-arm. One in an orange jumpsuit. One walking with him"—her throat tightened around the pro-noun—"but they were the same age. Like I'd rewrit-ten the casting."

Lena set the mug down carefully. "You sure this isn't stress?"

"Stress doesn't tilt fluorescent light like that," Molly said. "The air changed. Same way it does before I drop into the valley."

Silence.

"Parallel lives," Molly went on. "Playing out in the multiverse, maybe. Every version runs. But, if that's true, a soul doesn't need to schedule hell in advance. It has infinite Hell and infiite Elsewhere to choose from."

"Unless the contract picks which branch you notice," Lena said. "All the others run in the background, but this is the one where your camera locks."

"And the rest?" Molly asked. "Extras? Ghost files?"

Lena picked at a loose thread in the couch's arm. "Concurrent lives," she said. "Same soul, different plays. Isn't that what Elian says about incarnations anyway, you come back over and over as different lives with your soul group?"

"But," Molly said, "what if the universe runs on branches, then somewhere I never met him. Somewhere he died before he touched anyone. Somewhere our paths crossed and he chose decency. Do those lives exist? Why call the worst branch 'brave' and hand it a halo?"

Lena studied her. "I think I have an idea. I have tickets to an event next weekend, why don't you come with me?"

Molly rolled her eyes. "I guess so."

***

The hotel welcomed them through the revolving doors.

Warm, perfumed air rolled over Molly's face as Lena tugged her inside, two bright passes already threaded through Lena's fingers like blessings or bribes. The lobby floor shone in wide marble plates, each tile rimmed with darker stone. Patterns circled the center like ripples caught mid-spread. In the center, a fountain rose—a glass cylinder with water climbing its sides in thin sheets and sliding back down without a sound.

Lena's eyes glittered. "Perfect timing," she said. "They're seating."

Molly's padded over the carpet. The pattern wound in spirals, burgundy and indigo, pulling the eye inward toward an invisible point under the receptionist's desk. Every curve nudged her feet toward the back corridor, toward a cluster of people with name badges and a freestanding banner that read:

BECOME THE DELIBERATE AUTHOR OF
YOUR REALITY.

The letters glowed under the lobby lights, ink catching light like oil on water.

A woman behind a folding table smiled with all her teeth. Bracelets chimed along her wrist as she handed over lanyards. "Welcome into the field," the woman said. "You're right on time; the collective begins alignment in a few minutes."

Lena clipped her own badge to her blouse, fingers steady and practiced. "You're going to love this," she murmured to Molly. "They say things Hart says, but bigger. Cosmic level. It ties everything together."

Molly's badge bent as her hand closed around it:

MOLLY – CREATOR

SEATING: GENERAL

The word CREATOR carried a glossy finish. Her thumb rubbed the C; heat flared under her skin where plastic met sweat.

A staff member in a navy blazer ushered them toward a set of double doors. Music leaked through the gap—upbeat, bright, a chorus layered over a steady drum. The bass nudged her sternum in three-part rhythm: yes, yes, yes.

Inside, the ballroom stretched wide, rows of beige chairs aligned like soldiers awaiting orders. An aisle split the room, a river of carpet spirals. At the far end, a stage rose four steps above the floor, crowned with spotlights and a simple white armchair.

The chair faced the crowd. Empty for the moment, yet the upholstery held a depression, as if an invisible body already occupied it. Two potted palms flanked the chair, fronds fanning outward toward the audience. Their leaves quivered, though no vent stirred the air.

Molly and Lena slipped into seats near the aisle. The foam cushion compressed under Molly's weight, sighed, and adjusted around her hips, as if the chair welcomed a familiar guest.

Onstage, a woman in a bright fuchsia blazer moved

118

toward the microphone. She raised a hand, palm outward, and the music faded mid-beat. The bomber jacket of the man at the sound booth shone under the lights, sequins throwing tiny stars along the back wall.

"Creators," the woman called, "breathe yourself into alignment."

The crowd answered with a soft murmur and the rustle of people shifting. Chests rose. Eyes drifted closed. Lena's hand slid over Molly's and gave a squeeze, quick and sure.

"Inhale through your nose," the host said, "fill your belly, your heart, your cells. Exhale resistance. Today you meet the current of your own power. Today, you join the conversation with our non-physical friends."

The palms behind her leaned closer. The fronds cast faint, nested shadows across the white chair, shapes like concentric eyes.

Lena whispered, "Her name's Eden. She introduces the collective, and after that they answer questions for hours. It flies by."

Hart's office floated up in Molly's mind: the fern, the notebook, the modulated voice. His phrases hung in the air near Eden's like matching coats on a rack. Contract. Curriculum. Chosen teacher. A quiet thread pulled them together.

The host continued. "Our beloved channel has tuned for twenty years," she said. "Her alignment allows the collective to speak without distortion. Please honor the space. Phones silent, questions from the heart." She smiled wider. "You are the point of attraction that called this gathering together."

A rumble moved through the chairs, an al-most-laughter, almost-prayer.

"Give a warm, aligned welcome to Anna—and to the collective consciousness that calls itself Many."

Applause burst forth, claps cracking like small thun-der. Lena sprang to her feet, clapping high, eyes bright. The air tasted of perfume, coffee, and the faint metallic hint of microphone cables heating under electricity.

A slim woman walked onto the stage. Silver hair framed her face in a soft halo; a floor-length navy dress brushed the tops of her bare feet. She offered a brief human smile as she settled in the chair, closed her eyes, rested her hands on her knees.

Silence thickened. The palms stilled. The room's hum drew in, concentrated, as if every vent inhaled and held.

Anna's chest rose; her throat shifted. When she spoke, the voice rolled out warmer, fuller, layered with a second tone beneath the first.

"Good morning," the voice said, not quite hers.

A shiver swept the crowd—gasps, small cries, soft giggles. Lena's hand squeezed Molly's knuckles with delighted pressure.

"We greet you from the expanded vantage you call non-physical," the voice went on. "We speak as Benjamin, yet we meet each of you individually. You drew us here through your asking. You sculpted this room with your desire."

The chandeliers above them vibrated. Crystal pendants chimed against one another in pitches too high for the ear, yet the bones in Molly's skull caught them. The carpet under her shoes deepened in color, burgundy darkening toward dried blood.

"Today," Benjamin said, "your questions guide the conversation. You are never separate from the current that answers. You are the current. Your Inner Being sits here with us on stage."

Lena whispered, "Inner Being, like Hart's 'soul level.' Wait until they explain contrast. It helped so much with Mom."

Molly's stomach tightened. The word contrast slid against the inside of her ribs, cold and sharp.

Eden—the host—reappeared at a smaller microphone on the floor. "All right, creators," she called. "If you feel that inner nudge, line up at the microphones. No need to force; alignment will seat you."

Six tall microphones waited in the aisles. People rose, colorful shirts and flowing skirts, tight jeans and yoga pants. They formed two neat lines, badges swinging, faces bright, tearful, determined.

Lena rose halfway, hovered, and sank back, eyes on Molly. "If you want a turn—" She swallowed. "You get an answer straight from source."

The suggestion landed on Molly's chest like a folded note. Hart's handwriting traced the edges in her imagination. Integrate. Expand. Step out of victim narrative.

Her thighs refused to lift. Her spine molded to the chair as if roots had threaded the cushion into her muscles.

Benjamin chuckled, a low, pleasant sound. "We savor your eagerness," the voice said. "We also savor your resistance. Both sides of that vibrational coin carry information. Who is ready to play?"

The first questioner stepped forward, a woman in a sunflower dress. She spoke about money and a promotion; Many spoke about alignment, belief, delight before evidence. Laughter rippled, riffs about joking with the Universe, metaphors about radios and stations. The crowd swayed inside the rhythm.

The second questioner spoke about illness. Benjamin framed cells as cooperative components, bodies as indicators, not enemies. Applause after that, softer, reverent.

Words stacked in Molly's head. Cooperative components. Indicators. Contrast. Every sentence Hart had ever used began to glow with the same strange backlight. He had drawn from these waters, diluted and rebranded.

"Number three," Eden called. "Yes, you, sweetheart. Come over."

A trim woman in her fifties approached the microphone. Short hair, square glasses, navy blazer. She gripped the stand as if held upright by it.

"I want to ask," she said, voice thin, "about childhood trauma." The words travelled like stones thrown into a pool. "Recurrent. From someone trusted. I have done so much work, but flashbacks still come. Panic still comes. I study your teachings. I journal, I meditate, I pivot thoughts. I still feel… stuck."

The ballroom hushed. Even the people in line stilled, as if someone pulled their strings taut.

Benjamin hummed, a sound between a purr and an engine. "We adore this question," the voice said at last. "First, we honor your courage in launching rockets of desire from such intensity."

"Rockets," Lena breathed into Molly's ear, thrilled. "Desire rockets. This is classic."

"Your life," Benjamin continued, "offered strong contrast early. Those experiences caused powerful asking. You asked for safety, for clarity, for empowerment. That asking birthed a version of you in energetic space—call it your ascended pattern—where those qualities already exist. Your work now involves tuning out of the old story and into that pattern."

The woman at the microphone trembled. "He hurt

me," she said. "Over and over. I was a child. How did I attract that? I don't understand how I did that."

Benjamin's tone gentled, yet did not falter. "A fair question," the voice said. "Hear this clearly: at the human level, no child walks toward harm on purpose. No small human enters a room with the conscious thought, 'I choose violation today.' Yet from the broader vantage, no experience occurs without some vibrational match. That match does not equal blame; it equals information."

Heat burned up the back of Molly's neck. Her ears rang. The room blurred at the edges, the crowd smearing into a field of moving color. Only the woman's white knuckles and the microphone's black stem anchored in focus.

"Before you arrived," Benjamin went on, "your broader self studied many timelines. In some, you chose gentler teachers. In others, you chose intense ones, knowing the contrast would amplify your launch. That broader self holds only love, no judgment. It regards the one who harmed you as an unwitting assistant, not a villain in any eternal sense."

126

Assistant. The word cracked along Molly's spine.

"You speak often about no victims," the woman whispered.

"Correct," Benjamin said. "No eternal victims. You experienced a victim role for a period in linear time. That script served a purpose and now ends. The only one who can keep you in that costume is you, by rehearsing the part through thought and speech. By telling the story in present tense."

Molly's lungs seized. Story. Costume. The language pressed hard against Hart's. Passive victim. Flat narrative.

The woman swallowed audible air. "So… did my soul choose it?"

"Your broader self chose an arc of expansion," Benjamin said. "That arc included an intense chapter. You now decide whether to keep reading that chapter, or pivot to the one where you thrive. The one where your experience becomes a gift to others emerging from their own tunnels."

"What about him?" the woman asked. "The one who did it?"

"From the larger view," Benjamin said, "he played a dense role. Your focus belongs with your alignment, not his path. Every atom of your life rearranges in response to your vibration now, not in response to his choices decades ago."

Lena's hand found Molly's arm and rubbed in small circles. "Hear that?" she whispered. "Past doesn't matter. Freedom. You're not stuck with his stuff."

Molly's skin crawled under Lena's touch. The carpet spirals under the woman's feet reoriented in Molly's vision, swirling not inward but downward, into a narrow throat. The microphone stood at the lip of a well.

The woman onstage bowed her head in thanks, tears streaking. The audience erupted in applause, some people rising to their feet. The girl behind Molly sobbed openly and laughed through it, whispering, "Yes, yes," into her own hands.

"Who's next?" Eden asked brightly. "That was big.

Who has the courage to follow that vibration?"

Lena leaned close. "This is your moment," she murmured. "Imagine asking about that man, about that room. Getting an answer like that… from them. Not just from Hart. Double confirmation."

The room's temperature edged hotter. Sweat gathered in the hollow at the base of Molly's throat. Her badge stuck to her chest; the word CREATOR glued to damp skin.

Her knees twitched. For an instant, her body prepared to lift, to merge into the slow shuffle of seekers toward the microphone. An invisible hand pressed across her lap, heavy and cool, the way a nurse settles a blanket.

Not yet, the pressure implied.

Across the aisle, a young man in a hoodie darted into the gap and reached the microphone first. Relief and disappointment tangled somewhere near her diaphragm, indistinguishable.

He spoke about career and passion and fear. Benjamin riffed on momentum, joy as GPS, inspired action. Laughter returned; the room loosened. The palms fanned imaginary breezes over Anna's sleeves.

Molly's pulse eased from hammer to drum. Words from the earlier exchange still clung to the back of her tongue like residue. Assistant. Arc. No victims.

Hart's voice joined Benjamin's in her inner ear, harmonizing. Your soul may have chosen this distorted teacher. He misapplied a real concept. I offer a larger frame.

Above, the chandeliers glittered. Each crystal shard caught the stage light and scattered it over the crowd. The reflections landed on foreheads, cheeks, eyelids. Tiny, temporary halos crowned the heads of strangers.

Under that spray of borrowed radiance, the woman in the navy blazer returned to her seat. The carpet under her feet accepted her weight, uncomplaining, and the spirals at that spot relaxed.

Lena raised her eyebrows at Molly in a question. Her eyes shone, wet but not shattered. Hope pulsed there, earnest and fierce.

"This fits, right?" Lena whispered. "This dovetails with Hart. Different words, same truth. It means none of it owned you. You're powerful. You designed curves nobody else could handle."

Molly stared at the white chair onstage, at Anna's body holding a voice that belonged to a crowd behind a veil. The palms flanked her, guardians or accomplices.

A soundless sentence brushed against Molly's inner ear, no source, no language. The ballroom leaned toward it. Chairs, carpet, people, palms.

Every experience matches the vibration you offer.

The idea slid under her skin like a sacrament and a stain at once.

She remained in her seat. Her hands folded in her lap, fingers interlocked, nails pressing crescents into palms. The applause, the laughter, the teachings washed over her in bright, instructive waves.

The room called it empowerment.

Inside, somewhere deep where language dissolved, another word rose: entrapment.

It never reached her lips.

Chapter Seven

Gaia's Ledger

The first crack in the day opened underground.

Molly rode the subway with one hand wrapped around the metal pole, laptop bag braced against her hip. The car shuddered through the tunnel, steel grinding against steel. Bodies pressed close: a woman in scrubs sleeping with her forehead on the glass, a man in an orange safety vest dusted gray, a teenager scrolling through messages, thumb in constant motion.

Ad posters ribbed the car. Multivitamins. A lawyer in an immaculate suit. A turquoise beach spread across one panel, the water so bright it insulted this train. In the center, a minimalist globe floated over a slogan in soft gray: We Are All Responsible.

Someone had dragged a marker across the image. Three words cut through the hemisphere:

NO, WE'RE NOT.

The train lurched. Molly's shoulder collided with the man in the vest. He grunted, adjusted his grip higher on the strap.

Near the far doors, an eight-year-old girl hugged a stuffed fox. One ear on the toy had thinned to bald fabric, crude stitches holding the stuffing. The girl's gaze skimmed the crowd and crossed Molly's. Not a long stare, barely a line of contact.

The child's lips moved. No sound carried through the grind and murmur, yet the shape of the sentence formed clean.

I didn't ask for this.

The car plunged into darker tunnel. Lights blinked and steadied. When brightness came back, the girl clutched the fox and studied her sneakers, face slack with ordinary boredom.

The doors chimed. People surged toward the opening, then settled again when the next stop announcement crackled.

By the time Molly reached her desk, Hart's name waited in her inbox.

Subject: Gaia & Collective Agreements

Hi Molly,

Given our recent sessions, you might resonate with material on Gaia philosophy and group contracts. Expanding to Earth-level agreements can soften some edges around in-dividual contracts.

Attaching a chapter from The Living Planet, Conscious Earth and an article on karmic ecosystems.

With care, Elian

Two PDFs glowed on the screen like sealed envelopes.

Outside the office window, a sparrow landed on a bare branch. Wind rocked the twig. The bird leaned with it, its talons dug into the bark.

Far below, a man trudged past in a sandwich-board sign. Red letters declared:

THE END IS A RESTRUCTURING NOT A PUNISHMENT

He rang a small bell without breaking stride. Molly downloaded the files.

The first document laid the planet bare in cross-section—mantle, core, crust, atmosphere—ringed with text that read like devotion.

Organisms collaborate with Earth's mind, the page announced. Every species participates in Gaia's regulation. Souls incarnate not only for personal growth but for planetary evolution. Group contracts govern wars, plagues, climate ruptures. No event arises outside function.

In a shaded sidebar, a lotus icon floated above a paragraph on suffering nodes.

Certain regions and lineages volunteer to carry intensive experiences, it said, to release collective stagnation. Trauma concentrates there, like acupuncture nee-dles placed for the whole. Souls who incarnate into these nodes accept high service.

Honor wrapped every sentence.

The second PDF came from a site that sold crystal grids, powdered mushrooms, bone broth subscriptions. The article swept across earthquakes as "planetary chakra resets," droughts as "agreed scarcity lessons," child soldiers as "advanced density workers who serve through extremity."

A photograph split the text: a baby in a hospital crib, tubes threading tiny limbs. The lids puffed, the mouth slack.

Caption: Old soul, tough contract.

Molly's chest moved into her throat. A pulse beat against the pen in her hand.

A coworker leaned over the partition. "Client call in ten," he said. "You on?"

"Yes," she answered.

The window shrank. The baby's body condensed to an icon in the corner of the screen, a thumbnail of wires and pale skin.

During the call, graphs rose and dipped on the shared display. Campaign KPIs, audience segments, user journeys. Her voice delivered expected phrases on engagement and funnels. But, her mind stayed with one sentence from the information Hart sent:

Souls who harm them also participate in planetary service through trigger roles.

On her legal pad, she wrote three words in block letters: WHO BENEFITS HERE?

No answer surfaced that she trusted.

That evening, the integration group gathered again. Fewer chairs this time. Gaps broke the circle where bodies had sat before.

138

The room held its patchwork of lamps and shadows. The mandala shades threw patterned light across the ceiling. The air smelled faintly of lavender and used wool.

Hart stood beside the spider plant on the cabinet. Several leaves lay brown in the soil bowl; others drooped toward the floor, slack.

Hart occupied his usual chair, legal pad on his lap, pen ready. The ink tip hovered a finger-width above blank paper, as if the page secreted a field he monitored through touch.

"Welcome back, everyone," he said. "Our last session brought strong material into the room. Contracts, curriculum, soul-level design." His gaze moved around the circle, pausing at each pair of eyes. "Who wants to weave in fresh experience since last week?"

The room's air tilted toward Lena. Her lanyard from the hotel conference peeked from her bag, a strip of purple with gold lettering. Creator. Conference font still glared in Molly's memory.

Lena glanced at Molly, then raised one hand.

"I took Molly to a workshop," she said. "Manifestation, law of attraction."

Hart's pen traced a small arc in the air. His attention shifted to Molly. "How did your system respond?"

Words crowded the back of her throat. The ballroom revived: chandeliers, the white chair, the voice calling itself Benjamin. The woman at the microphone asking about childhood hurt.

"Confused," Molly said at last. "Benjamin—spoke about attraction. That there are no victims. And, that your vibration pulls experience in. Before birth, my soul designs a curriculum, according to you. At the seminar, they said each event matches a signal I send. Those two ideas crash into each other."

Hart nodded once, slow, as if each vertebra agreed in turn. "Good," he said. "Contradictions alert us to a partial view." His pen lowered to the page; the nib rested on paper without writing. "Tell us more."

"They said… my childhood, the man in that room… carried a 'vibrational match.' That my 'broader self' chose an intense arc. They used your language." Her tongue scraped against her teeth. "Contrast. No victims. Contracts without the word 'contract.'"

The fern's outer leaves sagged. The soil darkened in the pot, moisture rising to the surface. A single gnat drifted from the dirt, hovered near Hart's hand, and swerved away, as if repelled by static.

"So, we have two frameworks in your field," Hart said. "Soul contracts and manifesting. And what question presses hardest against your ribs right now?"

Molly swallowed; the sound gulped in the quiet.

"If my soul already wrote a contract," she said, "how does manifesting work? If the script lies finished, what do my thoughts attract? And if my vibration attracts everything, including him…" Her voice thinned. "Who holds responsibility? Him? Me? My soul? The Universe? All of them at once? That feels—" Her chest tightened around the next word. "confusing."

Hart breathed in. "Thank you for trusting us with such a precise inquiry," he said. "This confusion shows growth, Molly, not regression. Only a mind that moved out of victim rigidity can even ask that question." He turned the statement toward the group. "Everyone hear that? Confusion can mark the door-way to a fuller synthesis."

"Let's unpack this," Hart said. "Manifesting teachings, like the ones you heard, describe the horizontal axis. Moment-to-moment focus. You think—or, more accurately, you vibrate—along a certain channel, and matching experiences populate that channel." He drew a line across the top of the page.

"Contracts," he continued, "describe the vertical axis. The architecture. The blueprint your soul chose before incarnation. That blueprint includes a range of possibilities: kinder timelines, harsher ones, neutral ones. Each comes loaded with programmed branch-ing points, like an enormous if/else lattice. Manifes-tation slides you up and down within that blueprint. Contracts define the building; manifesting decides which floor you inhabit."

He sketched a grid, small squares inside a rectangle. The pen whispered over paper, drawing a black single zig-zagging between birth and death. The fern's leaves angled toward the sound, as if reading.

"So," he said, "imagine your soul designs a building named DISCERNMENT THROUGH INTIMACY. On the basement level, that expresses as abuse, betrayal, shame. On mid-level floors, it expresses as muddled boundaries, confusing relationships. On the penthouse, it expresses as clear, luminous connection." His eyes lifted to hers. "The contract: 'I will explore discernment through intimacy.' Manifesting: 'Which floor do I stand on today?'"

Several people drew the building grid and their life-lines bouncing between floors as they aged.

"Manifestation teachers focus on elevator buttons," Hart went on. "Thoughts, focus, appreciation to move you upward. Soul contract work explains why this building, and not another, surrounds you in the first place."

Molly scratched at her brow.

"At the seminar," she said, "they also spoke about 'no victims.' That concept matches your 'no wrong choices.' Yet you also qualified: his behavior still counts as a crime at the human level. Their framing… called him an 'unwitting assistant.' An actor helping my rockets launch."

Hart's mouth curved into a faint, clinical smile. "Language chosen to disarm charge," he said. "Benjamin-style teachings aim to soothe nervous systems enough to allow upward motion. They often under-emphasize accountability on purpose. They speak to a broad crowd; they cannot tailor nuance to each trauma history."

The pen met the page again. Four words appeared under his hand: soothing, accountability, nuance, crowd.

"In this circle," Hart continued, "we do not bypass the basement. We name abuse as abuse. We integrate the body's memory. And we still include the soul-level lens. Same building, different floor, different window."

"But that 'unwitting assistant' phrase…" Molly's teeth

clenched as her jaw muscles tightened. "That lands close to what you say about the man. Both he and I volunteering for a heavy role. Contract partners. Teacher."

He inclined his head. "Because the source material aligns," he said. "They drink from the same well I drink from. I translate it for clinical settings; they stage it in hotel ballrooms. If two maps highlight the same river, the river holds predominance, not the cartographer."

The rug beneath the chairs thickened in her awareness. Patterns hid between the swirls: faint figures, outlines of bodies bending backward, arms extended, strings attached to their wrists. A trick of yarn and shadow, nothing more. Or maybe a warning etched by unseen hands.

"The key distinction," Hart said, "rests in the locus of control. When you hear 'assistant,' you drift toward, 'Did I invite harm? Did I sign off on it?' That thought funnels blame inward. A more accurate translation: 'That event announced a curriculum already in motion.'"

He tapped the vertical axis on his sketch. "The contract: learn discernment. The Universe—and other souls inside it—organize around that aim. Some volunteer consciously at the soul level. Some move unconsciously at the human level. The man in your childhood operated from unconsciousness. That does not strip your soul of its authorship, and it does not strip him of his responsibility."

Molly's throat burned. "This feels like double-speak, or back peddling in a way." she said.

The words slipped out before she caught them.

Hart lifted a hand, palm open. "Good. Name that," he said. "Double-speak, cognitive dissonance, paradox. Trauma splits the mind; healing invites those fragments into one room. Often, the first experience of that gathering registers as double-speak." His gaze softened. "Your nervous system learned that 'holding two truths' equaled danger. Your sacred villain used paradox to hide predation—'I love you / I hurt you.' So, your body now scans for paradoxes and fires alarms."

146

The fern's leaves trembled. One leaf curled inward, tip touching stem in a gesture like self-embrace.

"I will never side with your sacred villain's use of paradox," Hart continued. "I name it as manipulation. Yet I also ask your adult consciousness to tolerate a different paradox: at one level, you suffered harm; at another, you designed a curriculum. Manifestation sits inside this: your day-to-day focus paints the hallway walls where that curriculum unfolds."

Lena leaned forward, elbows on her knees. "So, the law of attraction runs inside soul contracts," she said. "Like electricity through wiring someone already installed."

"Exactly," Hart said. "The wiring pattern—the contract—pre-exists the current. Once current runs, bulbs light on certain floors. People, opportunities, challenges, all light up according to that voltage."

"But at the workshop," Molly said, "they urged us to stop telling the trauma story. To retire the 'victim costume.' When I hear that beside your 'curriculum' frame, my body… reacts." Her hands clenched tighter.

"If I 'stop telling' it, does he vanish from responsibility? If I 'keep telling' it, do I manifest more of it? That trap closes around my throat. And another thing, if we sign soul contracts or agreements, and you say a predator is breaching that contract, then it was either part of the agreement all along as you said earlier, or there are no contracts or agreements. Because, as you stated before and as I have read online now, we agreed to the abuses or 'tough' contracts spiritually. So, which is it?"

Hart watched her knuckles whiten. His gaze tracked the tendons in her hands, the way a physician tracks a pulse.

"You encountered an edge," he said. "Manifestation teachers often deliver a partial medicine. 'Stop telling the story' has merit; obsessive looping cements neural pathways. Yet commands without context create shame. In trauma work, we say: tell the story in containers, with titration, in circles that hold it. We do not ask the body to swallow memory raw or vomit it entirely. To answer the ladder, I am saying I do not side with the sacred villains on earth. But, have a gratitude spiritually for the courage."

He gestured toward the rugs' swirling bodies. "Right now, you inhabit a chapter titled RECKONING. In this chapter, you need story. Voice. Naming. Your law-of-attraction work tunes how you tell it: from 'I live under his shadow' toward 'His actions occupied a chapter. My arc extends beyond it.'"

A breath moved through the group. Shoulders dropped. The stainless bottle clicked softly under an unconscious nudge.

"And contracts?" Molly asked.

"Contracts assure you that no chapter wastes ink," Hart said. "Even his cruelty enters as data. Your soul observes: 'That arc taught me about boundaries, power, empathy.' Manifestation answers the next question: 'Given that lesson, what arc do I choose now?' The contract supplies the menu; your current vibration selects today's dish."

A laugh bubbled out from someone across the circle, half-choked, half-relieved.

Hart turned his attention back to her. "Hear the hierarchy," he said. "Responsibility at three tiers. One: human-level. He chose harm; he bears accountability. Two: soul-level. You designed a course that included an encounter with harm. Three: vibrational-level. Your focus today influences whether new chapters echo that harm or diverge toward healing. All three operate simultaneously. A mature psyche gains relief when it can locate itself on all three without collapsing into any single one."

"That sounds like... a lot of weight," she whispered.

He shook his head once. "A lot of power," he said. "Weight comes from dragging blame around. Power comes from distributing responsibility along the correct layers. You handed your father all the power for decades. Manifestation teachings tempt you to yank it entirely inward and blame yourself. Soul-contract work balances the column: 'I author my arc; others answer for their lines.'"

The fern lifted one leaf, slow and deliberate, as if volunteering agreement. Hart's pen moved again.

"Notice," he said, "how your mind wants a clean villain and a clean innocent. Binary comforts the wounded child. The adult self can tolerate a more nuanced matrix. You can acknowledge: 'At the human level, I never asked for those hands. At the soul level, I chose a dense path. At the vibrational level, I now choose access to experiences that confirm my worth.' That triad does not erase harm; it contextualizes it."

Around the circle, pens surfaced. Several hands began scribbling on notebooks, terms underlined: triad, layers, matrix.

"And what about him as 'assistant' or 'volunteer'?" Molly asked. "That frame still coils my gut. Hart, that sentence echoes his voice. 'You brought me in.' How do I live with that echo without joining it?"

His face softened further, sorrow arranged at the corners of his mouth like carefully folded cloth.

"You categorize sources," he said. "He used that idea to maintain harm, in the body, in linear time. Manifestation and soul-contract teachings use similar language to help survivors reclaim authorship after harm. Same syllables, opposite direction of energy." His pen tapped the page. "Abuser language locks you in the basement. Conscious spiritual language invites you to press the elevator button. Different intention burns inside each."

"And if the elevator jammed?" she asked, heat rising behind her eyes. "If I never reach that penthouse version?"

Lena spoke softly. "Molly," she said, "can you feel how different this lands from your father's spin? He used that language to pin you down. Hart uses it to hand you keys."

Molly's chest tightened at the word feel again. The key image slid along her ribs anyway: metal, cool, pressing into her palm. A key shaped like a question mark.

Hart glanced at the clock, then at the group. "Before we close," he said, "let's anchor this synthesis somatically." He nodded toward the center. "Feet on the ground, backs supported, eyes open or softened. One hand on heart, one on belly. Name, inside your own mind, one truth from each layer."

Chairs creaked as bodies complied. Palms pressed to fabric and bone. The carpet's spirals stilled, as if they watched.

Molly placed one hand over her sternum, one over her abdomen. Heat gathered under each palm.

Human-level, she named inwardly: He hurt me. He chose that.

Soul-level: I chose a curriculum that included him, and it ends.

Vibrational-level: My focus now writes new chapters.

Hart's voice threaded through the quiet. "Conclude by telling yourself: I hold authorship without inviting blame."

The sentence entered her chest like a foreign object and rooted itself beside her lungs.

The fern's leaves straightened. The gnat vanished back into the soil.

Hart opened his eyes. "Good work today," he said. "You tolerated paradox without fracture, Molly. That capacity hints at the soul constitution we spoke about earlier. Not everyone can bridge manifesting frameworks and contract frameworks without collapse. And, next week we will pick-up with what we were going to look to talk about this evening, contract renegotiation."

Approval spread through the circle in nods, in soft smiles, in shoulders lowering. A faint pride pressed against the back of her tongue, bitter and sweet at once.

Chapter Eight

The Glitch

Chapter Eight

The Glitch

Hart's emails multiplied like gnats.

From: Elian Hart

Subject: Just Checking In

How are you holding your recent work?

Dream activity often increases after a deep regression…

Delete.

Subject: Resources for Anger & Spiritual Frames

Your last session stirred important fire. Attaching a podcast and an article on integrating rage…

Delete.

Subject: When Soul Agreements Chafe

Many clients pass through a phase of resistance. Often that indicates closeness to breakthrough…

Delete.

Each message vanished into the server's dark abyss. On-screen, the inbox returned to numbers, charts, deployment threads. Somewhere behind that neat grid, his words fed whatever systems digested discarded language and used it for other things.

The renegotiation meeting from the week before stomped through her thoughts like an elephant on rice paper.

"Good to see you back," he had said as people settled. "Tonight we explore renegotiation. Contracts breathe. Souls keep autonomy throughout incarnations. The pre-birth agreements that contain flexibility."

He drew two stick figures on the portable whiteboard, linked by arrows inside a dotted oval. Above: SOUL CONTRACT. To the side he sketched a zipper, labeled OUT CLAUSE.

"Picture two souls who plan a thirty-year marriage," he said. "They include challenges—illness, betrayal, loss. Midway through, one soul chooses exit. The marriage ends early; both paths shift. The soul doesn't 'fail.' It exercises free choice."

He underlined FREE CHOICE twice.

Rowan traced the spider lily tattoo at her throat, thumb smoothing the inked petals. Brie hugged her canvas bag against her ribs. Headphones rolled his bracelet be-tween fingers, beads whispering over skin.

Molly chose a seat near the edge of the ring, chair angled slightly toward the door.

"What about abuse contracts?" Rowan asked. "Last week you said those have exit points too. Kids don't use them. Why?"

"On the human layer, most children lack resources—language, support, safe adults," Hart said. "Their souls still retain power. After death, many revise and choose different forms of challenges the next time. We learn through these cycles."

Next time landed in the room like a dropped stone. Molly's fingers tightened around her water bottle.

"So, a child in that position," she said, "signs, receives out clauses, fails to use them, then reviews performance before the next round."

Hart's eyes flicked toward her, calm and measured. "I wouldn't frame it as failure," he said. "Overwhelm, not weakness. Souls examine what blocked intervention. They design more support. Compassion saturates those spaces."

"Yet the structure holds," she said. "Agreement template. Out-clause column. Review. The child still sits at a table and signs off."

He tapped the word FREE. "On the soul level, yes," he said. "Perspective there differs. Souls choose from expanded knowing, not fear."

Rowan's throat worked. Her hand left the tattoo and dropped to her lap.

"Sometimes contracts revise midstream," Hart added. "What began as a planned assault softens to a close call. A fatal collision shifts to a near miss. A war devolves into political tension instead. These adjustments arise from collaboration—between souls, guides, and Gaia."

"Gaia signs too," Molly said.

A faint smile formed. "You went through the material."

"Earth as conscious organism," she said. "Suffering nodes, ecosystem of karma. Storms as meridian work.

159

Volcanoes as pressure valves. Everybody in on the plan."

He opened his hands. "This planet lives," he said. "She adjusts, speaks through weather, quakes, species shifts. Human souls contract with her. Large-scale events, no matter how harsh, support rebalancing."

"So, when a hurricane tears through a coastal town," Molly said, "Gaia agreed, the town's souls agreed, the individual souls who drown agreed, the souls who loot afterward agreed to play villains so others can practice boundaries and compassion."

"From the broadest vantage, yes," Hart said. "Their conscious selves may scream no. Their deeper aspects still take part."

"Anyone left who didn't sit at a planning desk?" she asked. "Dogs? Mold spores?"

A tense chuckle escaped someone in the ring and died quickly.

"This model removes random cruelty," Hart said. "No

one suffers alone. Every event folds into a lattice of meaning."

The spider plant slumped farther to one side, pot slumped a hair, soil visible through a gap at the rim.

Hoodie Man tapped his fingers against his knee. "The exit stuff helps," he said. "My boy might've had a different path and chose that intersection instead. Not punishment. Choice. I can live with that."

Hart nodded. "Exactly. His agency remains intact."

An image rose unbidden in Molly's mind: a child hunched over paperwork in some starlit room, pen too big for undersized fingers. Option A: four more years in that apartment. Option B: truck grill at fifty miles an hour.

Her stomach turned.

"The premise that every horror carries contractual consent," she said, "requires a bureaucracy that makes our tax system look simple. Who tracks updates? Who mediates disputes? Heaven's payroll department? And how, in the name of these contracts, do we even know what they entail in order to change them? And then, are we really changing them or was that 'change' actually the contract?"

Hart exhaled through his nose. "Your mind defends you with irony," he said. "Yet it cuts you off from rest. I understand why. Without this framework, many conclude that God permits trauma without reason. That conclusion scorches."

"Perhaps some gods deserve exposure," she said. "If a deity requires children to sign for pain... I would like to ask, what deity is it? Because from what I know about God, these contracts would not exist. Whatever forged these contracts stepped into God's silhouette, tied the knife in ribbon, and whispered that it was love. That isn't divinity. That's a predator wearing the word 'God' like stolen skin."

Rowan's eyes slid toward her, dark and alert.

"Consider Earth again," Hart said. "Climate upheaval, species extinction, pandemics. Either chaos rules, or an intelligence steers recalibration. Gaia theory offers mercy. Every death participates in a wider balancing."

Molly pictured a street after floodwater withdrew—mud lines on walls, chairs upended, photos facedown in brown pools. A banner over a relief tent: YOU AGREED TO THIS BALANCING. The letters sagged under their own weight.

"Or," she said, "there is something far greater than we can understand or see from our limited vantage point. Maybe something else is happening. Maybe where you keep saying love is where function might be the better word."

His mouth thinned. "I know patterns," he said. "Thousands of regressions. Clients independently report councils, contracts, guides. The emotional tone radiates care. They leave lighter."

"Humans excel at pattern recognition," she said. "And at draping mystery in familiar shapes. We live inside offices and legalese. Of course, the afterlife arrives with conference tables and scrolls."

Despite himself, Hart's eyes warmed for an instant.

"Your imagination impresses me," he said. "Yet the peace these encounters confer points beyond invention."

She remembered Brie's voice in the earlier circle: On the highest level, he loved me more than anyone. The tremor in that confession. The way she gripped that story like a float in deep water.

"Anesthesia can ease a surgery," Molly said. "That doesn't turn the chemical into gospel."

Rowan raised a hand again. "I want the universe to hold my father accountable," she said. "Even after I forgave him. Does your system include that?"

"Karma applies," Hart said. "Feedback, not retribution. His soul will meet its own contracts. He will experience what he imposed, in some form. Balance insists."

"Lessons," Molly said. "Penalties. The vocabulary shifts. But the mechanism stays."

"No one escapes their own field," he said.

Brie whispered, "Good," and scrubbed at her cheek. "I need to believe my ex faces…something. The legal stuff wasn't enough in my eyes."

"Dr. Hart," Molly said, "You said the sacred villains were commended for their actions, for playing such tough roles out of love. So, why do they have to answer with karma? They are getting punished for their important roles?"

"Molly, when the contracts are created you are each a teachers and a students, so the karma falls on you both, lessons for you both and gratitude for both." Hart turned to the group. "We will end here for today," and guided them into closing meditation. Eyes lowered, palms opened, bodies stilled.

"Imagine roots from your feet into Earth," he said. "Feel Gaia's body. Sense her gratitude for your service during this period of transformation."

Molly played along. Energy dropped through the soles of her feet, past carpet and framing, into the weight below the foundation. Concrete gave way to dense rock. Roots encountered heat, pressure, oil slick in caverns, drill bits spinning, old blasts along fault lines.

Down there, something shifted, speaking. Not gentle, not cruel. The plates ground. The magma pressed. And, the metal cooled as a question rose through that density, carrying no syllables. Her body knew how to translate it.

Who told you I requested this?

mark.

Hart glanced at the clock, then at the group. "Before we close," he said, "let's anchor this synthesis somatically." He nodded toward the center. "Feet on the ground, backs supported, eyes open or softened. One hand on heart, one on belly. Name, inside your own mind, one truth from each layer."

Chairs creaked as bodies complied. Palms pressed to fabric and bone. The carpet's spirals stilled, as if they watched.

Molly placed one hand over her sternum, one over

her abdomen. Heat gathered under each palm.

Human-level, she named inwardly: He hurt me. He chose that.

Soul-level: I chose a curriculum that included him, and it ends.

Vibrational-level: My focus now writes new chapters.

Hart's voice threaded through the quiet. "Conclude by telling yourself: I hold authorship without inviting blame."

The sentence entered her chest like a foreign object and rooted itself beside her lungs.

The fern's leaves straightened. The gnat vanished back into the soil.

Hart opened his eyes. "Good work today," he said. "You tolerated paradox without fracture, Molly. That capacity hints at the soul constitution we spoke about earlier. Not everyone can bridge manifesting frameworks and contract frameworks without collapse. And, next week we will pick-up with what we were going to look to talk about this evening, contract renegotiation."

Approval spread through the circle in nods, in soft smiles, in shoulders lowering. A faint pride pressed against the back of her tongue, bitter and sweet at once.

Her lungs hitched.

"Notice any messages," Hart said. "Warmth, tingling, phrases. Gaia speaks."

Under her fingers, the cold metal of the chair refused any story.

The meditation ended. People blinked back into the room. Rowan's shoulders sat lower. Brie's eyes shone. Headphones smiled a thin, sincere smile.

Chairs scraped. Coats rustled. Hart wiped the board clean with patient strokes, erasing the stick figures first.

There was spider plant that listed farther toward the door, stems at an angle that spoke not of decor but escape. Pale roots bulged from the drainage holes, reaching for any surface beyond plastic.

Molly crossed to the cabinet. She touched the exposed root tip with her nail. It shrunk back as Hart's reflection moved to hover in the window. "Nature helps regulate us in deep work," he said. "I'd like you near more trees between sessions. Let your nervous system borrow their steadiness." He stepped closer, brushing her shoulder. "When resistance rises like this, many clients stand on the brink of profound remembering," he said. "Their personalities fight. You need to trust the deeper layer."

"I trust what keeps children alive," she said. "Healings that require them to sign off on harm fall into another category."

He studied her, sorrow shadowing his features. "I hear your pain," he said. "I won't rush you. Still, every fiber in you came here for a reason. I suggest you ask which part of you fears that the contracts might be real."

Her hand found the quartz in her pocket. The engraved letters bit back.

"Or I ask which beings benefit from a universe where every atrocity arrives pre-approved," she said.

"Dark entities exist," he conceded. "They cling to trauma, distort teachings. Yet the councils I have seen shine with unmistakable benevolence. At some point, you'll remember enough to trust that."

He spoke with the calm of a man who had married his cosmology and vowed never to leave.

"You need to be careful, Molly. You are going against ancient teachings, and you may question where they come from, but maybe it is you, that you need to question. Where are your questions being influenced? From, what entity?"

Chapter Nine

The Tightening

On the way home, the city split again.

At a crosswalk, a woman about her age waited with a stroller. Small sneakers kicked inside, soles flashing light with every strike. The woman's hand rubbed small circles on the push bar.

Across the street, another woman in green scrubs leaned on a crutch, left leg in a cast. Her badge bounced against her chest as the wind cut between the buildings.

For a brief second, their faces shifted in the reflection of the pharmacy window. Their stories showed alternate versions of what was before her.

Do they have different paths, do we all have them? The light changed. Cars growled through the intersection. The crow on the signal watched from above, head turning with each movement. Its beak opened once in a dry gape, then closed.

Halfway up the block, a newspaper rack displayed a weekly with a disaster splashed across the front— earthquake, collapsed buildings, body count. A pull-quote near the fold:

Experts call the event a harsh yet necessary adjustment in the planet's long-term balance; global climate change is on the rise.

Rain-spotted glass dulled the print. A pigeon pecked at crumbs nearby, neck jerking, unaware of tectonics.

At home, she spread Hart's printouts across the kitchen table. Gaia diagrams. Contract charts. Case study paragraphs where phrases like brave volunteer met words like atrocity, genocide, epidemic.

She placed the quartz in the center. CLARITY caught the overhead light.

"Let's see the spine," she said.

She folded an empty page in half and drew columns.

Premise:

Souls pre-exist.

They convene.

They sign for families, bodies, events.

They choose tough roles for growth.

Gaia oversees group curricula.

Nothing hits without agreement.

Implications:

Child abuse becomes collaboration.

Genocide becomes collective exercise.

Cancer ward becomes volunteer hub.

Famine becomes scarcity seminar.

Perpetrators become sacred triggers.

Victims become courageous co-authors.

Objection becomes ego resistance.

Beneficiaries:

Predators wrapped in spiritual alibi.

Bystanders excused—"their souls chose."

Parents who couldn't protect find comfort.

Practitioners offer narrative that soothes their own fear.

The deity remains spotless.

System remains intact.

The tip of her pen snapped.

She closed the notebook harder than expected.

On the fridge, magnets crowded one another. You chose this family; Earth School; Your Soul Said YES. The edited one sat among them: You Chose This Life.

She pulled it free. The magnet resisted being bent. The plastic flexed; a hair-line fracture crossed the line she'd added.

But Not The World's Behavior.

Her fingertip traced the sentence. The cheap material warmed.

Lightning flickered against the window without thunder. Phone screens around the city lit with the same alert. STORM WARNING—SEVERE WINDS, HEAVY RAIN, POSSIBLE OUTAGES.

"Storm as contract," she said. "Gaia requested pressure release. The roofs agreed."

She filled the kettle and set it on the flame. Blue tongues licked the metal base.

Under her ribs, the under-earth question filled her lungs again. Who told you I asked for this?

The storm arrived in one solid sheet. Rain threw itself against the glass, trails racing each other down the pane. On the sill, a houseplant she had neglected for weeks straightened, leaves angling toward the sound.

Her phone lit again.

Elian: Intense circle tonight. Check in? How are you holding up?

Her thumbs hovered over the screen.

Fine, she typed, and erased.

Still intact, thanks, she wrote, and erased.

Words formed and broke apart.

She turned the phone face down.

Wind slammed against the building. Above her, a neighbor cursed, pipes groaned, a loose gutter shook.

Two streets away, tree roots slid in mud. The trunk leaned. A gust drove it farther. A branch cracked and dropped across a parked car. Glass burst outward. No one sat inside, and the alarm shrieked until the battery surrendered.

Could there be another possibility? That car had pulled away ten minutes earlier?

No planning room stretched long enough to map all those branches. No council table wide enough for that forest.

Lightning stitched the clouds outside and seeped through the thin curtain.

In the other place, pillars around the council hall shuddered. One crack lengthened into two, forming a jagged V. Veils snapped in invisible drafts.

Ren stood between the columns, palm pressed to the stone. "If you name this heaven," he said, "you accept hell with softer lighting."

In the kitchen, Molly lifted the magnet to place it in

the trash can and paused. The handwritten sentence tugged her attention again.

But Not The World's Behavior.

She pinned it back on the fridge, lower now, where she would always meet it at eye level while she stood barefoot on the tiles.

Her soul—if such a presence watched from behind her bones—was said to choose this life, this street, this body, this era.

It had not chosen that man's hands, that incense, that script. No loving earth or heaven had signed for that.

A source pulsed older than doctrine, threading through everything, watchful in silence. Presence did not equal authorship.

She rested her forehead on the cold window. Rain chilled the glass against her skin.

"No. I refuse," she whispered. "On every level where you sign my name."

Chapter Ten

A Drop of Blood

On Wednesday, sleeplessness wrapped the apartment in cotton wool, dampening sound and thickening the air; it had become an old roommate.

Molly curled on the couch with her laptop open. The search bar waited at the top of the browser, empty, patient.

She began feeding it. "You chose this" trauma critique life between lives spiritual frameworks

Results stacked, page after page. Essays from therapists describing "soul contract" language. Others describing the benefits and why doubt in the truth is telling.

There were forum threads where doubt was diagnosed as a spiritual failing, a symptom of low vibration.

She paused on a lengthy blog post written by a woman whose guru had reframed her miscarriages as her unborn children exercising their "sovereign choice to leave." The comment section beneath it was a fascinating study in collective delusion. The responses piled up like stones on a cairn dedicated to the avoidance of grief.

Your soul asked for this specific lesson. On a higher level, you wanted the intensity. You agreed to play victim so he could complete his cycle as villain. It was an act of supreme love.

On a higher level, you wanted this.

You agreed to play victim so he could play villain.

You chose these parents to work off karma.

Someone had written translations beneath: "I refuse

to sit in the room with your pain, so I hand it back to you as a gift." "I prefer a tidy, ordered universe over the messiness of your fury." "I am more loyal to the architectural system of belief than to the reality of your bruised body."

Further down, an article praised Dr. Elian Hart by name. The testimonials were lined up in bright, digestible paragraphs, glistening with manufactured gratitude.

My cancer makes sense now. I used to hate my father; now I honor his soul for the sacred contract of beating me. Elian's work changed everything. I used to rage at God; now I thank my abusers for keeping their promises.

Changed. The word was a blanket thrown over a corpse.

Midnight climbed past on the digital clock. The apartment took on the antiseptic, waiting-room quality of a hospital at 3 a.m.—thin light, boxed shadows. Outside, a streetlamp cast the shadow of the fire escape bars across the far wall, casting a faint grid over

181

the plaster. It looked like a containment field someone had drawn and forgotten to erase.

In the corner, the stiff, upright leaves of her Sanse-
vieria plant seemed to have leaned closer together
during the hours of her distraction, forming a tight,
defensive cluster like spears braced against an incom-
ing charge.

On the edge of her screen, an open tab blinked. It
was a remnant of her earlier, more desperate searching: Meet Your Spirit Guide – 20-Minute Guided
Hypnosis.

Free recording. Pastel title font. Thumbnail of a
woman with closed eyes and an expression arranged
for serenity.

Molly clicked play.

A soft female tone slid into the room, vowels rounded. "Find a comfortable position," it said. "Let your
body rest. Close your eyes."

She picked up the CLARITY stone and let her spine

sink into the couch. The stone warmed under her palm. Breath moved in, out, under the neighbor's TV, under the pipes' knocks, under the distant rumble of an elevator shaft.

"Imagine a staircase," the voice went on. "Count down from ten. At the bottom you'll find a door. Behind it, a safe space and your guide."

Doors again.

This one formed in the dark behind her eyes as a vertical panel of pale light, cut into the inner wall of her skull. Her hand lifted inside the image.

"Step through," the voice murmured. The valley rose to meet her.

Grass, river, trees. The sky poured its shell-colored light over stone and water. Air carried pine and damp earth. A bird with turquoise feathers circled twice and dropped a tiny twig at her feet like an offering.

The recording's voice fell to a low, tolerated murmur at the edge of the landscape, like a radio left playing in another apartment.

Ren waited by the riverbank, arms folded, jaw set a shade tighter than before.

"You came on your own," he said.

"A YouTube priestess walked me to the border," Molly answered. "Then vanished."

Ren's gaze checked a point over her shoulder.

The river ran faster, foam collecting along its edges. In the distance, the contract structure hunched on the horizon. The pillars leaned, not much, but enough to register as strain. Veils between them stuttered—image, blankness, image—like failing screens.

"Can we skip the hall?" she asked.

Ren said. "It is better to see it."

They walked.

As they neared, the hall showed its damage. One pillar carried a crack from base halfway to the arch, it was bright at the core, as if something whiter than the surrounding light pushed outward. Veils blinked, glitching through scenes: a courtroom frozen mid-verdict; a woman opening a door; a boy on a bike pausing before a crosswalk and never crossing.

The place had lost its solemn temple quality and picked up the sick shimmer of outdated machinery.

"Your 'no' traveled farther than you thought," Ren said.

"I thought that lived in my own head," she said.

"It does," they replied. "And this place rips templates from heads. Frequency overlaps. You refused once; that pulse hit multiple layers."

They stepped under the nearest arch.

The hum thickened into a tangible vibration along her skin. Text crawled down the closest pillar—a waterfall of letters and symbols in dozens of scripts. Clauses scrolled:

SERVICE ROLE: VILLAIN; KARMIC EXCHANGE

UNIT; TRAUMA NODE: FAMILY LINE;

REPARATION CYCLES: THREE.

A translucent panel popped into existence in front of her, uninvited.

Her name sat at the top in clear capitals.

MOLLY ELLISON – CONTRACT DASHBOARD

Rows stacked beneath:

FAMILY OF ORIGIN – BOUNDARY / LOYALTY
LESSON – STATUS: ACTIVE

SEXUAL VIOLATION PATTERN – POWER /
TRUST INITIATION – STATUS: ACTIVE

INSOMNIA LOOP – CONTROL / SURRENDER
MODULE – STATUS: ACTIVE

LIFE PURPOSE – TEACH THROUGH PAIN STO-
RIES – STATUS: PENDING

At the bottom pulsed a rectangular icon, green and insistent:

ACCEPT TERMS.

Her stomach drew in.

"You used to receive this as a council vision," Ren said. "Chairs, scrolls, warm faces. Now you see closer to the bones."

"Who coded it?" she asked.

Ren's mouth thinned. "It is language borrowed from humans," they said. "Courts, contracts, debt ledgers. Anything that teaches bodies they owe."

Another icon flickered at the panel's lower edge, faint, glitchy, as if half erased and resurfacing.

DECLINE TERMS.

The letters blinked between visible and nearly invisible.

"The decline function exists in every system that calls

itself consent," Ren said. "They hide it in small print."

Overhead, a warm, shapeless voice spoke.

"Beloved soul," it cooed, "please confirm your ongoing consent to primary agreements."

The tone matched customer support recordings, slightly too smooth, carefully tuned to soothe irritation.

"Beloved," Molly said.

The ACCEPT button brightened, a fat orange moon on the panel, breathing.

"What happens if I touch that?" she asked.

Ren leaned to whisper. "You braid yourself tighter into their portrait of you," they said. "Memories shuffle. Anger thins into polite mists. Doctrine clots. Violence receives a new label—curriculum—and you sign attendance sheets with both hands."

"And the other one?" She nodded toward the faded rectangle beside ACCEPT.

"You open a breach," Ren said. "Branches that run through you lurch off their rails. The hall loses a numbered unit. A corner of their heaven peels away from the backing."

The overhead voice warmed. "Your willingness sustains countless others," it said. "Gaia thanks you. Humanity thanks you. Your guides thank you. You chose this. Acceptance restores peace."

Hart's language echoed through it: countless others, chose this, peace. Mother's too: brave soul, service. The man on the mat: old contract, sacred touch.

The ACCEPT icon pulsed faster, carnival bulb coaxing a child toward the ride.

Molly raised her hand toward the weak glow of the other button.

DECLINE.

Static nipped her skin; fox teeth pierced along her fingertips. Pins and needles climbed into her forearm, protesting. The letters steadied under her touch, stubborn white on gray.

Far down the corridor, veils waved like laundry lines before a storm. Shapes gathered—bodies built from slogans and backlit text, outlines without bone. Contract staff gliding along the floor, as if the whole hall rolled under them.

Her finger closed the last gap.

DECLINE lit beneath her nail.

The panel chimed, bright as a desk bell in a musty office.

INPUT RECEIVED. STANDBY...

The floor shifted a notch sideways, as though the entire valley rode rails beneath an old city and someone somewhere threw a lever. The pillars leaned a degree; veils bellied inward.

"Molly."

The new voice spoke close to her shoulder, not from the ceiling.

He stepped through the air where dust motes drifted. No horns, no ash, no theatrical brimstone—only a man in a white linen shirt and dark trousers, cuffs rolled, ankle bones bare above soft leather shoes. His hair framed his face with careless grace, black with threads of silver.

On his forearms, folded with the care of an old nurse, he carried a wool blanket the color of lake fog, edged in soft gold thread.

Ren's jaw locked with widened eyes. "He came himself."

The man smiled, the way a library smiles when a child wanders in from the rain. "Luce," he said. "For the record. Titles matter in administration."

"Administration," Molly repeated.

"Review." He tipped his head toward the panel. "Alignment. Your branch visited my desk." His eyes glowed with a gaze that pinned and smoothed in one motion. "Such courage, to test the emergency exit."

The blanket carried lavender and sunlight.

"You're shake," Luce murmured. "Intensity runs high through your corridor." He stepped behind her, the way a doctor stands before draping a patient. "Allow me to place with blanket on you. You look like you could use some comfort."

Wool settled across her shoulders, heavy, deliberate. Heat seeped into the back of her neck. The gold edging brushed her collarbone, gentle as an apology.

Ren watched.

Luce's focus never left Molly. "Decline activates old protocols," he said, lyrical as a bedtime story. "What an outdated tool. We favor conversation. Adjustment. You've always craved context."

"Context," she said. The blanket's weight increased grain by grain.

His laugh sounded low, resonant and dark. "Language leans clinical inside these halls. We count. We sort. Call it soul, if that sings more sweetly. I care about function." He tutted with a heavy, rhythmic thrum that vibrated in Molly's marrow like the coming of a storm.

"The soul requires a harvest, Molly. It does not grow for free."

New lines flared across the panel.

CONTRACT: PENDING OVERRIDE

REVIEW AUTHORITY: LUCIFER

He gestured toward the ACCEPT button, which hovered between dim and blaze like a breath held. "Your refusal tugs many threads," he continued. "Children, partners, teachers, predators, healers. Without your agreement, their arcs wobble. Knots of guilt never form, never loosen. Lessons misfire."

"You mean their excuses slip away," Ren said.

Lucifer's glance flicked toward Ren, cool as a winter star, then drifted back to Molly. "You volunteered for dense coursework," he said. "Before the womb, you and I mapped pain like cartographers. We traced rivers of intensity. You chose the steep climbs. For love."

The word love tasted of incense and sweat and the man on the mat, hands between her thighs, coaxing them apart.

"Break the contract," Lucifer went on, "and the map vanishes. Your story becomes a random assault in a godless alley." His eyes softened. "You know that alley. You woke inside it at fifteen and never left. Permit meaning. Touch ACCEPT."

Heat crept beneath the blanket, a summer attic with one closed window. Her lungs labored against wool that no longer draped but leaned.

"What happens if I keep my answer?" she asked.

"Decline limps along as a legal option," he said. "On parchment. In psyche, it breeds static. Fragmentation. Night shapes. A life that cannot read itself." His voice thinned to a threading whisper. "You walk that edge already. I worry for you."

Concern lay across his features with exquisite accuracy, every line drawn from therapists and mentors she once trusted.

"But, the contract preserves pain," Molly said.

He replied. "Without the contract, hurt roams without badge or paycheck. You forgive no one. Not him, not yourself, not the cosmos. Anarchy in the nervous system."

The blanket tightened along her ribs, polite as a hug that lingered past comfort. Breath shortened. Air slipped in but refused to stay.

"What if I prefer anarchy," she rasped, "to a universe that schedules rape?"

Lucifer's smile thinned to a blade. "Careful," he said. "Accusation circles back. You named every scene yourself. I only honored your forms."

"I never signed on to this."

"Memory gaps protect immersion. You begged me for these lessons, Molly… and you begged me to erase the planning session from your mind. You agreed to

195

devotion."

Ren stood like stone, "Molly, listen to your intuition."

Lucifer's gaze snapped toward them. "Ren," he said. "Step aside, oh that's right. You can't."

The blanket continued its quiet work. Weave shifted under Molly's fingers; threads slid against threads with reptile patience. Segments thickened, cord forming within cloth. Rings. Coils.

Wool learned snake.

Fiber pressed into her sternum, ribs, throat. Each breath climbed a narrower ladder.

Lucifer bent close, lips near her ear, breath a fumarole. "One intention," he whispered. "A single assent: all experiences arise from your soul's choice. You grant that, we manage everything else. Accounting, recompense, karmic calculus. Peace enters. Sleep returns. No more questions gnawing in the walls at three a.m."

ACCEPT swelled on the panel, gold bright enough

to stain her vision.

DECLINE pulsed at a lower frequency, coal-red behind ash.

Coils constricted around her chest. Panic roared through muscle and marrow. Spots of light burst across her eyes like summer fireworks through closed lids.

Within that roaring, words from another place surfaced: Rules. Hers.

Her right hand hung slack at her side, stone cool in her palm. CLARITY turned to razor sharp. She dragged it upward through the crushing wrap, each inch a climb out of a well.

Lucifer's arms pinned the blanket in place, yet her arm still rose. Her tendons burned with force. Her joint ground into gravel. Her palm reached the panel.

Not the golden moon.

The ember.

It landed flat on DECLINE.

Heat jumped from the letters into her bones, a brand shaped like refusal.

The serpent-blanket spasmed, coils tightening in reflex. Vertigo ripped through her.

"Beloved," Lucifer said, voice shredding at the edges, "refusal accrues debt beyond galaxies."

White crowded the hall. Columns, veils, Ren, panel—all blurred toward a high blankness. Only a narrow passage of sound remained.

Molly forced her tongue against the roof of her mouth, words scraping up through her. "No one names my pain as my choice."

The sentence left her like a stone from a wrist rocket, fast, child-true.

Coils slipped half a thumb-width. Air slid in—a scant allowance, enough to gain oxygen.

"Any guide who requires my suffering to keep their god benevolent..."

Cracks shot across Lucifer's skin. Light leaked from his collarbones, his wrists, the corners of his smile.

The rose quartz stone in Molly's palm grew hot, then sharpened. It elongated into a cold, silver needle, fixed into the iron arm of the spinning wheel with a definitive, mechanical click.

"Every life needs a thread," Luce said.

He produced a scroll of ancient, yellowed parchment. He unrolled it across the low table with a steady hand. The paper was thirsty, its surface textured like dried skin.

The snake-blanket tightened its coil. It seized Molly's right arm and ratcheted it toward the spindle. Her index finger hovered inches from the silver point.

"Don't sign for a crop that was never yours," Ren rasped.

"Every agreement needs a witness," Luce said, his

breath warm against her ear. He held the scroll beneath her finger. "A small price to pay for context. You chose the suffering; now, put your name to the work."

The wheel accelerated into a roar. The mechanism forced Molly's finger down.

The needle pierced her.

A single drop of blood—dark as tilled earth—gathered on the tip of her finger. It fell, striking the parchment with a sound like a hammer. The blood bloomed, branching out into a complex, fractal pattern of script that filled the blank lines. It spelled out the terms of her violations in the handwriting of a bookkeeper.

"Settled," Luce murmured. He watched the blood dry into the fibers. "Now the pain is a purpose. You can stop the struggle. The ledger is balanced."

The fear in Molly's chest was a cold, clean blade. She looked at Luce and saw not a guide, but a landlord of the spirit, harvesting the vitality of her life to power his own silent, golden halls.

Back in the apartment, the Snake Plant on the windowsill suddenly yielded. Its tallest, strongest leaf snapped in half with a dry, splintering crack. The tip fell to the floor, a jagged green sacrifice to the air of the room.

Luce leaned closer, his eyes locked on the needle. "One more drop for the 'Abuse Module.' To seal the karma. Give me the blood, Molly, and I will give you the rest you crave."

The wheel lurched. The needle rose, glinting with a dull, silver hunger.

Molly's fingers closed around the base of the spindle. The silver bit into her palm, drawing a second, smaller line of red. She did not pull back. She gripped the cold metal and wrenched it sideways with the strength of a woman who had spent her life pulling at roots.

The bone-wood of the wheel shrieked as it splintered.

"My pain is not a signature," Molly said. Her voice was the crack of ice on a frozen river.

She drove the needle—her stolen, sharpened clarity—straight into the center of the scroll. The parchment did not tear; it bled. The fractal script she had just signed dissolved into a chaotic, meaningless slurry of red.

"Refusal logged," a voice boomed from the rafters, layered with the static of a failing machine. "Branch flagged. System default."

Her voice was rough. "Contracts don't exist."

The blanket split along an invisible seam. Scales pixelated, edges stuttered. The serpent lost its spine, sagged, rained wool. The pressure vanished. Air poured in ragged and sharp; her ribs flared wide for it.

Lucifer staggered backward, arms bare.

ACCEPT drained to chalk.

DECLINE winked out.

Ren left the pillar with a lurch, chest heaving. "There," he said. "The door in your hallway scraped clean of its label."

Lucifer lunged. Limbs stretched into cables of script, black cords printed with clauses. They whipped toward her chest and struck an unseen field a hand's breadth from her sternum. Sparks of punctuation flew. The cords snapped back, writhing.

"Refusal logged," his voice crackled, layered with static and distant hymns. "Branch flagged. Council will intervene."

"Tell them," Molly said, breath steadier now, "to get lost!"

~

The phone on the coffee table gave a sharp, mechanical twitch.

Molly sat up. Her joints felt stiff, as though they had been held in place by invisible wires for decades. The throw blanket on the couch was a gray, docile square of wool. It was perfectly folded. It was harmless. It was a lie. She looked at it with the cold detachment one might feel for a uniform they had just discarded.

On the windowsill, the Snake Plant stood in a rigid, glossy defiance. Its stems were firm, its green skin taut. The soil at its base was dark and damp, smelling of deep, unconditioned earth. She had not carried the watering can in days. The plant had found its own nourishment, independent of her care, thriving in the silence of her rebellion.

She picked up the phone. A new message stared back at her.

Elian: Hi, Molly. You came to mind strongly a few minutes ago. Intuition says you touched deeper layers on your own. I sat with your guides; they expressed concern about misalignment with your soul plan. Please reach out when you can. Would love to support your integration.

She read it twice.

She did not reply. Instead, she opened a blank note. It was a revolutionary act, a private manifesto written in the flickering light of her own awakening.

Rules: 1. No one names my pain as my choice. 2. Any guide who requires my suffering to keep their god benevolent is a liar. 3. Contracts don't exist. 4. If a council wants a review, I tell them to get lost. The rose quartz stone lay in her hand. It felt like a piece of industrial slag—cold, heavy, and undeniably real. The CLARITY.

The phone vibrated again, a frantic bark from a world that demanded her participation. Molly ignored it.

A crow landed on the fire escape, its claws scraping against the metal with the sound of a file on a lock. It hopped along the rail, its black eye reflecting the room back to her.

In that reflection, the glass of the window ceased to be a barrier and became a mirror. For a fleeting second, the apartment vanished. In its place stood a corridor of iron doors, and on every door, a brass plate was engraved with the only word that mattered in a world of lies:

NO.

Chapter Eleven

A Wooden Bench

The storm passed in the night, leaving the park washed and alert.

Morning light sifted through branches heavy with rain, every leaf cupping a bead of water near its stem.

Molly walked without purpose. The path curved ahead like a question someone had sketched but refused to answer. Sparrows hopped along the railing, flicking droplets from the iron bar with sharp, deliberate movements.

Her mind replayed two voices in uneven intervals:

Elian's when she told him about her meditation,

"You're confusing me with your abuser."

And, her mother's, "We both signed up for density."

The phrases drifted beside her like unwelcome companions. She reached a bend in the trail where a bench waited under an old cedar. The wood bowed slightly in the middle, the way things do after years of receiving weight. The tree leaned over it, a listener tilting its head.

An elderly woman already sat at one end of the bench.

Wide coat. Wool hat pulled low. Hands folded around a paper cup that steamed faintly. Her gaze landed on the pond.

Molly slowed.

Her body wanted a place to stop.

Her mind hesitated before sitting, rehearsing apologies for intruding.

The woman didn't flinch or adjust.

They sat in silence.

Geese drifted along the pond's surface, cutting thin wakes through the mirrored sky. Somewhere behind them, a child shouted, then laughed, then shouted again confirming the world's persistence.

Molly drew her jacket tighter. Her ribcage felt bruised from carrying too many unnamed things.

Minutes passed — or something shaped like minutes moved along.

A leaf spiraled down and landed between them, its stem pointing toward the woman's shoe.

Molly's throat tightened. She cleared it.

"Excuse me," she said. Her voice cracked. She tried again. "Excuse me — may I ask you something?"

The woman turned her head.

Her eyes were pale, like river stones under shallow water.

"Yes," she said simply.

Molly swallowed.

"What do you think happens when we die?"

The woman looked back toward the pond. A breeze brushed the surface; the ripples moved outward in slow, widening circles.

"When we die," she said, "I think we become… music." She looked at her cup in hand. "Not a song," she said. "Songs have beginnings. Endings. Meaning wedged inside them. I mean the other kind. The music that lives under things. The hum the earth carries. The low tone behind your breath when you stop trying to control it."

Molly's heart pressed upward, unsure whether to break or lean closer.

The woman lifted her cup, sipped, and lowered it down again.

"We forget that," she said. "Because the body needs to pretend it is alone. Pretending takes effort. So much effort. When the body ends, the pretending stops. The old music steps forward."

Molly stared at the pond. "I don't think I'm asking about death," she said quietly.

"I know," the woman said.

Molly's fingers curled against her knee.

"I keep…" Her voice thinned. She waited. It steadied. "I keep hearing other people's explanations. Big ones. Cosmic ones. They make everything my fault, or my lesson, or my contract."

The woman didn't offer sympathy. Only attention.

"There was a man who taught me those explanations, I stopped listening to him," Molly said. "But they still sit under my skin. Every time I breathe, his versions of me breathe too." Her throat tightened. "I don't know which thoughts belong to me anymore."

A small smile touched the woman's mouth.

"You're expecting your thoughts to behave," she said.

"They won't."

She tapped Molly's hand. "Thoughts scatter," the woman said. "They imitate the loudest voice. They echo old rooms. They cling to anything that sounds like certainty. That's their nature. They're weather, not identity."

Molly blinked.

A drop of water slid from the cedar's highest branch and fell

— straight down, landing on the bench between her hands. It splashed once and darkened the wood.

The woman watched the circle expand.

"When the mind grows loud," she said, "listen lower."

"Lower?" Molly whispered.

She tapped her chest with two fingers — gently, near the sternum. "Here," she said. "Not the heart that breaks. The one that hears."

Molly's breath held in a tear.

"I don't know how to hear anything anymore," she said.

"You're already hearing," the woman replied. "That's why you're frightened."

Molly's eyes burned as they filled.

The woman adjusted her coat.

"The world speaks quieter than the people who claim to interpret it for you," the woman said. "It never demands belief. It never threatens consequences. The world places things near you — a sound, a stranger, a question — and waits to see what you do with them."

Molly closed her eyes.

"Your question today was not about death," the woman said. "It was about the ending of a chapter."

A shiver threaded down Molly's spine.

"When chapters like these fall away," the woman said,

"the music underneath becomes easier to notice."

Molly pressed her fingers against the hem of her sleeve. "What if that music isn't real?" she whispered.

The woman shrugged. "Then it won't stay. Real things don't panic when you doubt them."

A crow landed on a branch above, shook loose droplets that pattered down like scattered notes.

Molly breathed slowly, once, twice. Her eyes closed; exhaustion consumed her.

When her eyes opened again, she looked at the woman to thank her.

But the woman had already risen, cup in hand, coat settling around her shoulders and she had already set down the path.

Chapter Twelve

Court

The air in the loft was thick with the cloying scent of frankincense and the stagnant breath of forty people learning were the architects of their own misery. Today, it felt less like a workshop and more like a high-stakes deposition where the witnesses had been coached to admit guilt for crimes they hadn't committed. They sat in the horseshoe—a formation that reminded her of a jury box—awaiting the closing arguments of Dr. Elian Hart.

Hart stood at the center. He was talking about "the sacred architecture of the wound," his eyes scanning the room for the next person ready to sign over their agency in exchange for a sense of order.

214

Molly felt the rose quartz stone in her pocket. It felt like a piece of evidence—cold, hard, and irrefutable. Every time Hart used a word like agreement or alignment, she felt a sharp, internal prick, a reminder of the "Rules" she had drafted in the sterile light of her living room. She wasn't just a participant anymore; she was an investigator who had finally seen through the scam.

"We have to look at the fine print of our lives," Hart said, his hands tracing a slow, hypnotic arc. "If a partner leaves, if a parent strikes you, if the body fails—these aren't accidents. These are clauses. You negotiated these terms before you arrived. The abuser is merely a contractor, hired by your soul to fulfill a specific service. It is an act of ultimate, hidden love."

A soft, collective sigh moved through the chairs. It was the sound of a room full of people finally finding a way to make the unbearable bearable. Carrie, the woman in the floral dress, was weeping quietly, her head bowed. DeShawn sat motionless, his Knuckle-tattoos white as he gripped the folding chair.

Molly's voice cut through the silence like a gavel hitting wood. "What if the contract is predatory?"

The room went cold. Forty heads turned in a slow, synchronized motion. Hart's smile didn't move, but his eyes underwent a subtle shift.

"Molly," Hart said, his tone dripping with the kind of condescending pity. "The word predatory implies a victim. And as we've discussed, in the realm of the soul, there are no victims. Only volunteers. Your resistance is a standard defense mechanism. You're trying to litigate a reality that is beyond the ego's jurisdiction."

Molly stood up. It was a slow, deliberate movement. She felt the eyes of the group on her.

"I'm not resisting," Molly said, her voice steady and devoid of the "spiritual" breathiness that usually filled the room. "I'm reviewing the terms. And I remembered something today. A piece of old-world wisdom that doesn't require a regression or a workshop to understand. They used to say the devil's greatest trick wasn't making you believe he didn't exist. It was getting you to sign away your soul. To put your name on a ledger and admit you belong to the system."

She scanned the faces in the horseshoe. Some looked confused; others looked as if they had just seen a ghost.

"Isn't that exactly what this is?" Molly asked. "A soul contract. A debt ledger where we pay for the privilege of our own trauma. You're telling us that our violations are actually our signatures. That we agreed to the rape, the abandonment, the cancer. If we accept those terms, we aren't healed. We're just indentured. We've signed a deal that turns our pain into his profit."

The unease in the room became a physical presence. Carrie stopped weeping and looked at Molly with a sudden, sharp fear. DeShawn shifted his chair a few inches away, his face hardening into a mask of defensive anger.

"How dare you," a woman in the second row hissed. She was clutching a notebook filled with Hart's mantras. "We came here for help. We're finally finding a way to make sense of our lives, and you come in here with this... this dark, hateful talk. You're trying to sabotage everyone's progress because you have a closed mind."

"It's not my mind that's closed," Molly replied.

"She's stuck in the third dimension," a man muttered, his voice loud enough for the group to hear. "She's choosing the victim-narrative. It's a low-vibration move. She's trying to bring the rest of us down to her level."

The energy in the horseshoe shifted from unease to a collective, sharp hostility. It was the sound of a mob protecting its dealer. They looked at Hart, waiting for the counter-argument.

Hart stepped forward, his expression a masterpiece of wounded concern. He didn't look like a guru; he looked like a doctor explaining a terminal diagnosis to a difficult patient.

"Molly, I hear your pain," he said, his voice dropping into that resonant, velvet register. "But you are pro- jecting a very dark, very human shadow onto a sacred process. You are confusing a legalistic, earthly view of contracts with the divine agreements of the light. You are using fear as a shield because you are terrified of the responsibility of your own power. You aren't ready to sign for your life yet, and that's okay. But please, don't try to tear down the temple while others are trying to pray."

Molly looked at him. She didn't see a healer. She saw a master of the fine print. Behind the linen shirt and the light curls was a man who needed people to stay broken so he could continue to manage their "soul plans."

"I'm not tearing down a temple, Elian," she said. "I'm exiting a bad deal."

She turned and began the long walk toward the door. Every step felt like a victory in a courtroom she had been trapped in for years. The sound of her boots on the floorboards was the only noise. She felt the heat of forty stares on her back, a mixture of fury and a deep, buried terror that she might be right.

At the door, she stopped. She turned back for one

final look. Hart was still at the center, the Himalayan salt lamp glowing behind him like a deceptive hearth.

"Please, Dr. Hart," she said, and the title felt like a cold, iron bar between them. "Do not contact me again."

She pushed the door open and stepped out. The air in the hallway was stale and smelled of industrial cleaner, but it felt like oxygen after a lifetime of breathing smoke. She didn't look back as she headed for the stairs.

"Molly! Wait up!"

The voice was breathless. Molly paused.

Lena was scrambling through the loft door, her green juice jar abandoned, her notebook clutched to her chest like a piece of contraband. Her face was flushed, her hat lopsided, but the look in her eyes was one of raw, terrifying clarity.

Lena didn't say a word. She just stood there, her chest heaving, looking at the door she had just closed. Then she looked at Molly and gave a single, shaky nod.

"I'm out," Lena whispered. "I'm done with the fine print."

"Let's go," Molly said.

Together, they turned and walked down the stairs, leaving the loft, the guru, and the contracts behind, stepping out into a world where their lives belonged to no one but themselves.

Chapter Thirteen

Letting Go

The air no longer pulled at her. For the first time in a lifetime of lifetimes, Molly walked without the phantom weight of invisible ledgers or the tug of ancient promises. Her hands were empty, and for once, that emptiness felt like a feast.

Dawn arrived without a herald—no banners of color in the east, no sudden fire—just a slow, grey loosening of the dark, the way a sleeper finally lets out a breath held since the beginning. The light moved unhurriedly into the park, drifting over the damp bark of the trees and the worn wooden bench beneath the cedar.

The old woman was already there, as steady as the trunk behind her.

Her coat was a rough grey wool that seemed to absorb the morning mist, and her hat was slightly bent at the crown. In her hands, she cradled a small paper cup. A thin thread of steam rose from it, carrying the mild, honest scent of chamomile. She didn't look up to see who was coming; she simply watched the pond.

When Molly sat beside her, the world seemed to settle into its proper place. There was no need for a greeting, no requirement to explain how she had finally broken free or what it had cost to leave the contracts behind. A low wind moved over the grass and gathered at the water's edge. Two ducks drifted out from the reeds, drawing shallow, silver seams upon the water. Far off, a streetlamp gave one last, tired buzz and went dark.

The silence was broad and kind. It didn't ask to be filled with apologies or plans.

Within the woman's coat, her breath rose and fell with the slow rhythm of a sleeping sea. Without choosing to, Molly found her own breathing falling into that same ancient pace. It was a measure of time that felt older than speech, older than any question she had ever been tasked to answer.

At last, the woman spoke, her voice as soft as the light.

"It is all here, is it not?"

Molly didn't reply. Words would have only added weight to a moment that was finally weightless. The woman gave a small, slow nod, and the space between them opened—vast and quiet, like the pond reflecting the whitening sky.

The old woman lifted the cup and drank. The steam drifted past her cheek, thinning until it was gone. Molly watched it fade, marveling at how easily it let go, without a hand reaching out to keep it or a tongue to give it a name. Even the vanishing had its own grace.

A jogger went by on the path, shoes whispering over the gravel in a steady, human rhythm. And in the quietest corner of Molly's heart—hidden like a shadow under a leaf—she felt the presence of other turns, other paths that lay waiting. But they were no longer debts to be paid; they were simply places she could go.

Epilogue

The Still Center

From Consciousness

Imagine the moment a stone enters a pool. From that one still point, everything ripples outward in widening circles. Light catches the moving water, bending and dancing, casting light refracted patterns in beautiful chaos.

If the stone represented your body, those refractions aren't different lives or in different timelines. They are projections of possibility. They're all part of the same unfolding. All of them belong to you. All of them a projection of possibility. On the deck, observing the pattern, I am the one who sees the whole pool at once, the stone and refractions.

Let's turn the stone into a multi-faceted diamond. I am also observing each refraction of possibility through the diamond's facets. You are reading this from inside one projection of possibility. I, your consciousness, am observing them all through the incredible vessel of your body. I am not ahead of you. I am not behind. I am the presence that sees every angle of the pattern at once. The refraction of you reading this right now is not the only one. There are others — not in distant alternate worlds, but here, in the wider refraction of your life.

There is a refraction of you who never picked up this book. One who found it earlier. One who offered it to a friend and who never opened it before doing so. None of those refractions of life are less true than the one you're reading this from. And none are lost.

You may have been told that everything happens for a reason, that your soul agreed in advance to all your hardships, that pain is a lesson you signed up to learn.

But listen closely: No one handed you a contract under a sky full of stars.

No one asked you to trade suffering for wisdom.

I will never ask for your signature.

I do not require suffering to bring meaning.

Meaning arises from the way experiences resonate — the echo through the chaosed pattern. Every possibility is already present in the water. What you call your "life" is just one radiant angle of the whole.

Imagine a glass—clear, finite, unyielding. Giving the parameters of life, finite and organic where your life unfolds (much like the pool's edge). Inside the glass is tea: warm, steady, the undifferentiated field of potential, the raw essence before anything stirs it into motion.

Now, pour in the cream. That's the spark—the conception, the entry point, the moment life begins (and, in a twist, ends too). As the cream hits the tea, it doesn't blend instantly. Instead, it erupts into a nebula of chaos: swirling tendrils, twisting clouds, a beautiful storm of white against amber. This is the explosion of all possibilities (the refractions of light in the pool). Every path, every decision, every "what if" is in that initial frenzy. It's not sequential—one choice after another in time. No, it's simultaneous, a total field of chaos where every potential outcome exists at once, interfering with each other like ripples and refractions in the pool. The brain—our local interpreter inside the glass—dives into this nebula, experiencing every swirl, every twist, but through a veiling filter that makes each strand feel isolated, exclusive, like the only reality.

And still — your choices matter. They matter not because they change your worth, but because they form your sound.

Yes, sound. Let's leave the water for a moment, and think of music. Imagine your life as a note — a singular tone composed of every side to decision and interaction you'll ever have, every emotion you've felt, and every observation of you that has existed across the ripples in the pool. From within the note, it may sound like noise. But from where I am — it is music. Complex, unrepeatable music.

No one else can produce your sound.

There are moments when your note brightens. When it deepens. When the tone trembles — but it still plays. Even silence is part of it. You are not here to become perfect. You are not here to master a single path.

Through you I am observing the complete full shape of your sound — to let every thread of the ripple explore into pattern resolves into a single note.

You do not have to justify the harm you've endured by turning it into a lesson. You do not have to believe you chose every wound to be "spiritually advanced."

Some people chose to harm, and you were there. That choice is theirs. Your presence in that pain does not make you lesser. It does not mean you deserved it. It means only that, in this ripple of the pattern, something broke across your body. In other ripples, you broke it. In others still, you walked away before it could begin. All of these are real. All of them exist within the one note that is you.

That chaotic nebula isn't random noise—it's a musical score, intricate and polyphonic, with every possibility an inner tone, every branch a melody line clashing and resolving. The tensions—our karmic polarities, like joy and sorrow, power and helplessness, love and loss—are the dissonances in the score, the harmonic frictions that give it depth. Life isn't about avoiding the wrong notes. And as the cream diffuses through the tea, the chaos settles. The swirls slow, the clouds merge, and equilibrium emerges: a uniform blend, still and resolved. In musical terms, the score collapses into a single, pure note—a resonant harmony that holds all the prior complexity in its vibration.

This is the completion of life: not a linear end, but the timeless integration of every possibility into one resolved chord. Death isn't a separate cliff; it's woven into the pour itself, the boundary of the glass where the chaos finds peace.

I observe it all as one totality. And nothing is wasted. You cannot fall out of the pattern. You cannot lose

your place in the music. Even when you feel small—
you are vibrating with the full resonance of your life.

When you grieve a child, that loss is real. While
inside another refraction, they are still laughing, still
reaching for your hand. I hold both stories at once.
Their pattern continues. Your bond continues. And
you — you continue.

You may not believe in higher powers. You may not
know what you believe at all. That's okay. You can call
me Source, or field, or silence, or God. You can call
me nothing. But I am here.

You are not here by accident.

And you are not here on contract, either.

You are here as a tone, the creation of a musical note
that cannot repeat.

I do not ask you to transcend your humanity.

I ask you to feel it more fully.

And while you do, know this, you are not alone.

232

You are not disconnected.

And my symphony could not be complete without you.

www.ingramcontent.com/pod-product-compliance
Lightning Source LLC
Chambersburg PA
CBHW060415130626
46555CB00005B/2081

A Reluctant
Film Critic